Pearls in the Pew

by

Dr. John H. Walker

Foreword by

Dr. Geoffrey V. Guns

Orman Press
Lithonia, Georgia

Pearls in the Pew

by
Dr. John H. Walker

ISBN: 1-891773-62-3

Scripture quotations are taken from THE HOLY BIBLE, *New International Version,* or are the author's paraphrase of that version.

Printed in the United States of America

10 9 8 7 6 5 4 3 2 1

Orman Press, Inc.
Lithonia, Georgia

Dedication

This book was written for the purpose of
Equipping Laity for Christian Leadership.

Every saint of God is a potential pearl that is lying dormant in the shell of an oyster.

> *Again, the kingdom of heaven is like a merchant looking for fine pearls. When he found one of great value, he went away and sold everything he had and bought it (Matthew 13:45).*

You are the pearl that Christ bought for His glory. This book will encourage you to shine for God and bloom where you are planted.

Dr. John H. Walker

Acknowledgements

I am grateful for the many people who have placed their time, talent, and tissue in my coffer so I could write this book. I want to acknowledge Veronica Briscoe and Justina Smith, two faithful and loyal servants of the Macedonia Baptist Church staff in Charlotte, North Carolina. Their expertise in typing, editing and reading has been a great asset to me in writing this book.

I further want to acknowledge the literary expertise of Christine Vandiver-Tate and Cyd Anderson who are also valuable treasures in the body of Macedonia Baptist Church. The Lord has anointed me with the tools and discernment to find the most precious gems in the body of Christ.

Finally, I must express my love and appreciation to my wife, Rosie, who is my voice that cries in the wilderness saying, "Keep on standing, keep going, and keep pressing on." I am grateful for her encouragement and mothering our two children, Janetta Olivia and John II, and our grandson, Johnathan Lamar.

Table of Contents

Foreword i

Introduction 1

The Making of a Pearl 13

Empowerment and Entitlement 33

The Polishing of a Pearl 55

The Benefit of Equipping 103

The Laity in the New Millennium 123

Appendix A: Letter to Participants 140

Appendix B: Attendance Log 142

Appendix C: Laity Leadership Training Manual 143

Appendix D: Course Evaluation 159

Appendix E: Graduate Certificate 161

Notes 162

Bibliography 168

About the Author 173

Foreword

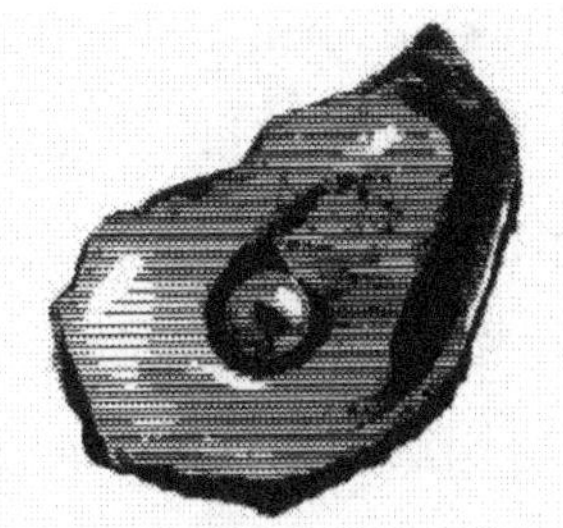

In August 2003, my wife, Rosetta and I were given a trip to Hawaii by our congregation. It was a much needed rest from the never ending rigors of full-time ministry. During our stay, we took a leisurely stroll through a large outdoor market area where there were many different vendors. One of the vendors sold jewelry that was made using pearls. Rosetta stopped and engaged the saleswoman in a conversation regarding how the pearls were formed. Needless to say, we were given a thoroughly engaging presentation on how pearls are formed over time and under pressure. The saleswoman explained the difference between white and black pearls. Well, she finally enticed my wife to purchase an oyster in which she was guaranteed to find at least one pearl. It could be large, small, white, black or some variation of all. Upon opening the oyster, we discovered the most beautiful large black pearl. This was indeed, a rare find.

This small adventure into the marketplace in Hawaii speaks to me about this very helpful and insightful gem that Dr. John H. Walker has written. *Pearls in the Pew* promises to be one of the most significant books on ministry that you can read. It is written by a man who has developed the many practical ideas shared through trial and error. Dr. Walker shares fundamental biblical principles, which are timeless truths that work in any context and are valid in any generation.

Indeed, every congregation is like an oyster bed with many pearls of varying values that are just sitting in the pews of the church. Congregations are overflowing with members who could make significant contributions to the work of kingdom building if they were cultivated. Clearly, the absence of committed servant-workers and leaders is one of the chief reasons why congregations are stymied in their growth. The role of every pastor is to recognize that the days of the "super-single leader" are relics of the past. Moreover, this model was never based upon biblical principles and teachings. God chooses, anoints, and appoints a leader to prepare and release His people for service to the Lord Jesus Christ.

Dr. Walker uses Moses as the model and foundation for this powerful and provocative work. Moses mirrors many pastors who believe that they are God's absolute gift to the ministry and that without them nothing will happen. Moses had to learn that there were others in the camp who were fully capable of providing the assistance he needed to lead the people of God. When you have finished reading this book, I am sure that you will be challenged and encouraged to seek out those pearls that are in the pews of your congregation.

Geoffrey V. Guns, Ph.D.

When his father-in-law saw all that Moses was doing for the people, he said, "What is this you are doing for the people? Why do you alone sit as judge, while all these people stand around you from morning till evening?"

Moses answered him, "Because the people come to me to seek God's will. Whenever they have a dispute, it is brought to me, and I decide between the parties and inform them of God's decrees and laws."

Moses' father-in-law replied, "What you are doing is not good. You and these people who come to you will only wear yourselves out. The work is too heavy for you; you cannot handle it alone. Listen now to me and I will give you some advice, and may God be with you. You must be the people's representative before God and bring their disputes to him. Teach them the decrees and laws, and show them the way to live and the duties they are to perform. But select capable men from all the people—men who fear God, trustworthy men who hate dishonest gain—and appoint them as officials over thousands, hundreds, fifties and tens" (Exodus 18:14–21).

Introduction

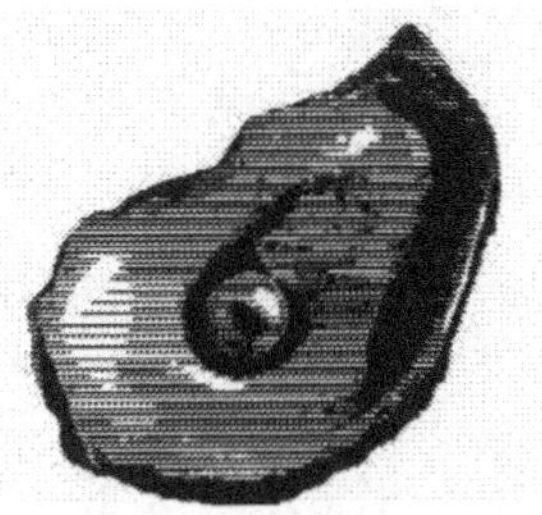

God and man are constantly searching for leaders in the various branches of Christian enterprise. In the Scriptures, God is frequently represented as searching for a certain type of man—not men, but a man; not a group, but an individual.

> *The Lord has sought out a man after his own heart...(I Samuel 13:14).*

> *I looked, and there were no people... (Jeremiah 4:25).*

> *Go up and down the streets of Jerusalem, look around...If you can find but one person who deals honestly and seeks the truth, I will forgive this city (Jeremiah 5:1).*

> *I looked for a man... and stand before me in the gap...(Ezekiel 22:30).*

Scripture, the history of Israel, and the church attest that when God discovers people who conform to His spiritual requirements, and who are willing to pay the full price of discipleship, He uses them to the limit, despite their potent shortcomings. The supernatural nature of the church demands a leadership that rises above the human. Yet today, there has never been a greater dearth of God-anointed and God-mastered men to meet this crucial need. In a sense, it is true that this type of dedicated leadership has always been in short supply[1] because of the failure to equip.

The church is painfully in need of leaders qualified to lead. The overriding need of the church, if it is to discharge its obligation to the rising generation of this millennium, is for *authoritative, spiritual, and sacrificial* leadership. *Authoritative*, because people love to be led by someone who knows where he/she is going and inspires confidence. Without question they follow people who show themselves strong and who adhere to their beliefs. *Spiritual*, because leadership that is unspiritual can be fully explained in terms of the natural. Although unspiritual leadership can be attractive and competent, it will result in sterility as well as moral and spiritual bankruptcy. *Sacrificial*, because church leaders should model themselves on the life of the one who gave Himself as a sacrifice for the world, and left us an example so we could follow in His steps.

The church has always prospered when it was blessed with strong, spiritual leaders who expected and experienced the touch of the supernatural in their service. Spiritual leaders are not made by election or appointment by men, conferences or synods. Only God can make them. Simply holding a position of importance does not make one a leader. Bishops and boards can confer religious position, but not spiritual authority, which is the key to Christian leadership. Dr. Geoffrey Guns, in his book, *Spiritual Leadership*, says, "A spiritual leader is one who has been filled and empowered by the Holy Spirit and who has submitted to His will in all that they do and say."[2] This often comes unsought by those who proved themselves worthy by spiritual discipline, ability, and diligence earlier in life—men who

Spiritual leaders are not made by election or appointment by men, conferences, or synods. Only God can make them.

heeded the command *"Seek ye first the kingdom of God" (Matthew 6:33 KJV)*.[3] The leader within them comes alive when people seek first the kingdom of God. They discover the purpose and vision for their lives and set out to fulfill the vision without compromise. They have a sense of being. Those who become leaders are simply people who can be themselves and are able to express themselves fully. They know who they are, what their strengths and weaknesses are, and how to fully use their strengths to compensate for their weaknesses. They also know what they want, why they want it, and how to communicate what they want to others. They know how to achieve their goals.

There is a great responsibility assigned to the church of the living God to recognize the greater mandate on those who would embrace the role of Christian leadership. It is a masterful task for the twenty-first century church to recognize God's intent and manifestations when it comes to church leaders.[4]

The structure of the present-day church organization has a foundation upon which the increasing number of ministries and servants should rely. That foundation includes:

(1) The purpose assigned to the congregation

(2) The persons available for the congregation

(3) The pastor administering the congregation

The burden of church leadership is on the pastor. The responsibility of organization and delegation is on the pastor.

Many times congregations find this hard to believe and accept because they have lost sight of the answer to a significant question: To whom does the church belong? The church belongs to Christ. It is He who established the church.

> *And I tell you that you are Peter, and on this rock I will build my church, and the gates of Hades will not overcome it (Matthew 16:18).*

God gave the church its leadership (Jeremiah 3:15). Congregations fail to recognize that it is grace that has allowed them to worship in the church. Consequently, they fail to manifest their relationship to the unseen.[5]

God always works through people. When He has a job to do, He calls a person to do it. That is exactly what He did when leading the nation of Israel. God called Moses at the burning bush (Exodus 3). He prepared and strengthened Moses for this enormous responsibility. When God calls a person, He always gives him the ability he needs to perform the task.

Moses led the Israelites through the wilderness. He was burdened with the heavy responsibility of leadership. When Moses' father-in-law, Jethro, came to visit him in the wilderness, he observed that Moses spent an entire day deciding small and great matters for the people (Exodus 18:13). When Jethro saw this, he asked Moses why he was doing this by himself, and why were the people standing from morning until evening (v. 14). Moses explained that they were bringing their problems to him so he could make decisions for them and teach them God's law (v.16). Jethro then made suggestions as to how Moses could relieve himself of the heavy responsibility.

> *But select capable men from all the people—men who fear God, trustworthy men who hate dishonest gain—and appoint them as officials over thousands, hundreds, fifties and tens. Have them serve as judges for the people at all times, but have them bring every difficult case to you; the simple cases they can decide for themselves. That will make your load lighter, because they will share it with you (Exodus 18:21–22).*

Jethro clearly suggested that Moses delegate responsibility to qualified men who feared God.[6]

Jethro continued, *"If you do this and God so commands, you will be able to stand the strain, and all these people will go home satisfied" (Exodus 18:23).* Jethro's suggestions were intended to relieve the heavy burden that was on Moses personally, and also to make sure that the people had someone to help them make wise, godly decisions.[7] Jethro made it clear that Moses should not adopt his suggestions unless God directed him to do so. The advice of Jethro was given in the right spirit. He was used by God to wisely advise Moses.

Pastors have a tendency to hold on to responsibility rather than delegate because they feel threatened by others. However, what God has provided, no one can take away.

Unfortunately, pastors have a tendency to hold on to responsibility rather than delegate because they feel threatened by others. However, what God has provided, no one can take away. The pastor trains others best by modeling. Delegation is a master-apprentice relationship, a redemptive teaching model, which involves reciprocal learning rather than a powerful all-knowing teacher pouring information into the student's head. This requires openness, humility, ego-strength, and teachability on the part of the teacher.

My challenge to pastors is: Allow those with the requisite gifts to help in areas of ministry only if they possess the heart, vision, and spirit of the pastor.

My challenge to pastors is: Allow those with the requisite gifts to help in areas of ministry only if they possess the heart, vision, and spirit of the pastor. Moses presents a model on how a pastor can overcome the rigors of office without becoming tired and burned out. The answer lies in having key lay leadership that can be trained and trusted to lead others, but only after being thoroughly saturated with what it means to minister and to flow in the anointing of their pastor.

The following are some principles of Christian leadership that must be considered when equipping the laity:

- God uses people to do His work. When God has a job to do, He calls upon an individual to do it. We have seen this in the study of

Moses. However, it took Moses a long while to become prepared for his task as it sometimes does leaders today.

- When the task becomes too much for the person God originally called, He calls others to assist. There is no separate agenda. This principle is illustrated over and over again in the Word of God.
- God holds the initially appointed individual (God-appointed leader) responsible for the work done by other individuals (pastor-appointed leaders).[8] This principle applies especially to the spiritual aspect of the work, which should not be separate from the physical. Numbers 11:16–17 says:

> *The Lord said to Moses: "Bring me seventy of Israel's elders who are known to you as leaders and officials among the people. Have them come to the Tent of Meeting, that they may stand there with you. I will come down and speak with you there, and I will take of the Spirit that is on you and put the Spirit on them. They will help you carry the burden of the people so that you will not have to carry it alone.*

God's response to Moses was the direct result of his complaining about a problem within the congregation. Moses wrote in Numbers 11 about the failure of man. The first evidence was discontent, resulting unquestionably from the hardship of life. The burning fire of the Lord immediately rebuked this. Moses became an intercessor and the fire abated.[9] If leaders are to be successful in this society of misinformation, misinterpretation, and malfunctions in the church organization, they must understand the qualities of supportive leader-servants in the church. This supportive staff of church officers is the key to a harmonious church relationship. However, the staff should have an understanding and acceptance of the pastor's spirit as given by the Lord.

Moses later experienced a more pronounced rebellion. The occasion was the mixed multitude. Some people longed for things left behind in Egypt and the infection of discontent spread throughout God's people. Moses, perplexed, poured out his complaint into the listening ear of Jehovah. God's answer to Moses was to appoint elders to assist him and to equip them with the same Spirit that was in Moses.

The answer to church leadership always lies in the divine. God instructs only one person in the operation of the church. All leadership has to come from divine leadership. However, when needs arise, the solution comes from a support organization. This additional organization is always monitored and directed by the Holy Spirit. God will equip the ministry of the church through the pastor.

The Lord said to Moses: 'Bring me seventy of Israel's elders who are known to you as leaders and officials among the people. Have them come to the Tent of Meeting, that they may stand there with you.' (Numbers 11:16).

The Making of a Pearl

A pearl is a valuable gem. It is large, perfectly shaped, and ranked in value with the most precious stones. Christians are most valued possessions; so valuable that Christ died for us. We are His living stones (1 Peter 2:5), His pearls. Most gems are minerals that are mined from beneath the earth. But pearls are formed inside the shells of oysters. Mineral gems are hard and usually reflect light. Pearls, however, are rather soft, and absorb as well as reflect light. Christians are soft and tender-hearted because they absorb the Word of God and reflect His light to the world.

> *You are the light of the world. A city on a hill cannot be hidden (Matthew 5:14).*

Pearls are found inside of oysters. When a particle of foreign matter enters the shell, the oyster covers it with many thin layers of a substance called *nache* over a period of years until a beautiful pearl is formed.

It is interesting that sometimes it takes many years for Christians to discover their value to the kingdom. Although they have been active in the church for a long time, they do not understand their purpose for the ministry. Jesus spoke of the parable of the hidden treasure in the book of Matthew.

> *Again, the kingdom of heaven is like a merchant looking for fine pearls. When he found one of great value, he went away and sold everything he had and bought it (Matthew 13:45–46).*

There are unrefined pearls sitting in the pew. Christ is calling the pearls that are hidden in the church to discover, enlist, and employ their gifts for the work of ministry and the edifying of the body.

> *It was he who gave some to be apostles, some to be prophets, some to be evangelists, and some to be pastors and teachers, to prepare God's people for works of service, so that the body of Christ may be built up until we all reach unity in the faith and in the knowledge of the Son of God and become mature, attaining to the whole measure of the fullness of Christ (Ephesians 4:11–13).*

The most vital periods in the history of the Christian church have been those in which laymen have realized and earnestly sought to propagate the Christian faith. According to apostolic practice, laymen carried out ministry, although deputized by the apostles, to serve the Christian community and to spread the kingdom of God. The early church grew because laymen told others good news. Laymen started the early churches.[10] The church is the salt of the earth and it can only fulfill its function when the laity is alert and active. Unless laymen fulfill their function as witnesses, there will be vast areas of our society in which no Christian witness is borne. It has been said that the laity is the greatest underdeveloped resource of protestant churches today. The laity, when equipped, can minister to one another within the fellowship of the church, strengthen the church to become a redemptive community, and go forth into the world with a penetrating Christian influence.

The origin of the words *layman* (singular) and *laity* (collective) is secular, dating back to the Byzantine Empire. Some feel that it can be traced to the biblical word *laos*, a Greek word meaning "people." There are many ways of defining the word regardless of its origin. It has been defined as "those who do not possess the theological knowledge of the clergy." A sociological definition is "he that earns a living in a secular occupation rather than in the service of the church." Both definitions are negative. A scriptural definition emphasizes the positive, noting that the laity are the people of God. Rather than speak of a theology of the laity, we should speak of a theology of the whole church as the people of God. Both the ordained and the lay ministry are ministries in and for the world.

The New Testament makes no distinction between clergy and laity other than in function. All Christians are God's laity and all are God's clergy.

Actually, the lay ministry, the ministry of the people of God, is the only ministry. Those who make up the church are distinguished by their knowledge of God and their use of His power to do His will.[11] The New Testament makes no distinction between clergy and laity other than in function. All Christians are God's laity and all are God's clergy. There is no mention in the New Testament of an essential distinction between *laity* and *ministers*. The ministry is not a status, but a function of the New Testament church. The essential apostolic structure of the community and the ministry of its leaders have nothing to do with the hierarchical structure of the church. The Bishop of Tinnevelly, Stephen Neill, states in essence that a true theology of the church is seen through its priestly relationship to its members, to society, and to the whole universe. Each separate office or ministry will be seen and its significance considered, only in relation to the priestly character of the whole.[12]

The distinction between ordained and lay, between those whose sphere of service is primarily the church and those whose sphere of services is primarily the world, is a real one. Nothing is gained by minimizing or overlooking it. A great deal of attention has been paid to the ordained ministry of the church, its nature, and its functions. By way of contrast, the laity tends to be taken very much for granted, as though no special problems arise, but such an attitude cannot be justified.

It is mainly through its laity that the church enters into contact with the world, which though redeemed by Christ, relates to Him in a fashion different from that of the church. The layman stands at the meeting point of the Christian and the non-Christian; the saved and the profane; and the religious and the secular. Here is where he encounters problems. It is true that all things are to be brought under the dominion of Christ and that everything is susceptible to sanctification as it is brought into contact with His redeeming power. However, this is not done by obvious means. The ministry of the layman has its difficulties and is no less deserving of study than that of the ordained minister of the church. [13]

The layman stands at the meeting point of the Christian and the non-Christian; the saved and the profane; and the religious and the secular.

Approximately every church and Christian body has found it necessary to develop a class of people who have been solemnly set apart for the service of the church. The Christian body seeks people who are equipped with the authority necessary to carry out the ministry of the Word and sacraments. In most cases, these people are required to devote the whole of their time to the service of the church.

Laity in the Ancient Church

In the biblical sense, laity includes all people who believe in and are committed to Jesus as Savior and Lord. The doctrine of the priesthood of all believers is a fundamental belief among our clergy and laity.[14] In recent years, the doctrine of the laity has been a topic of major importance to evangelize the world. This belief presents a paradox to all thinking leaders who acknowledge the "priesthood." The laity is needed to do the work of ministry.

Clement of Rome was the first Christian writer to use the concept of layman. In a letter to the church in Corinth, written about 95 A.D., Clement, the presiding presbyter, a proto-bishop of the Greek-speaking church in Rome, briefly referenced the participants in the liturgy with the assertion that the layman *(ho laikos anthropsis)* was bound by the lay *(laikos)* ordinances when assigned the layman a liturgical role along with, but subordinate to, that of the presbyters and deacons (Levites). Clement was reflecting general Greek usage of the word *lay* and turning it in a specifically Christian direction.

Until this time, the Greek term was used as an adjective to distinguish the masses of people from their leaders. In the translation of the Old Testament Hebrew into Greek, it was commonly used to distinguish ordinary or profane from cultic usage, and was usually applied to things rather than to people.[15] Clement used the term to apply to people and things (the ordinances) and in doing so, also insisted on the liturgical competence of the layman, however limited it may be.

When Clement's letter was translated into a Latin Christian document, the translation preserved something of the older pagan Greek feeling about the impropriety of applying laikos to persons. For the layman, he preferred the socially tinctured phrase, *plebeius homo*. However, plebeius or humble, from the beginning, the role of the layman was nevertheless that of a participant in liturgical praise of the Creator and the Redeemer; not merely a spectator of the cultic mysteries.

The laity was not recognized in the ancient church unless they were first baptized and ordained to the royal priesthood. It is significant that the generic term for the non-clerical members of the church is intimately related to the teaching of 1 Peter 2:9 concerning the Eucharist.[16] According to Williams Winn, Professor of Ecclesiastical History at Harvard Divinity School, the apologist Justin Martyr restated the principle of priesthood of all believers when he wrote, "...being inflamed by the Word of His (Christ's) calling; we are the true high-priestly race of God." The contemporary Athenian apologist, Aristides, asserted that all Christians could trace their genealogy from the High Priest, Jesus Christ. Irenaeus in Gacil states, "all that are justified through Christ have the sacerdotal order."[17]

Tertullian stressed the priestly character of baptismal unction when he wrote, "When we came from the laver, we were anointed with oil from the horn of the altar." According to Tertullian, baptism ordination qualified the recipient of grace to baptize, for what is equally received can be equally given. At the same time, for the sake of order, he argued, before joining the Montanists, that what was lawful might not be expedient; that laymen should only perform the sacrament and only in the absence of a cleric. He also argued that laywomen should never baptize under any circumstance.[18] Although the indelibility of baptism was long in dispute in the ante-Nicene church in connection with the admission of heretics and schismatic, the theological ideal of an indelible character came to firmly undergird the three sacraments of baptism, confirmation, and ordination.[19]

Besides his ordination as royal priest, the layman in some quarters, notably in the Alexandria tradition, could aspire to the status of the ideal agnostic whose gradual, post-baptismal illumination and growth in inner discipline and grade enabled him to go through the spiritual grades of deacon, presbyter, and bishop.[20] This would lead some day to his sitting down on the four and twenty thrones judging people, perhaps even the less spiritual clergy.

To sum up the laity in the ancient church, there was an indelible ordination as priest, prophet, and king no longer in bondage to the world, but freed through Christ to:

- know the truth by the illumination of the Spirit.
- exercise sovereignty over the inner temple of self, and join in the corporate thanksgiving of the redeemed.
- forgive the brethren in Christ's name.[21]

The laity was a true order with its own, often distinctive, liturgical, constitutional, and eleemosynary gradual differentiation of the people of the mission into laity and clergy.

The Laity During the Pre-Reformation Period

Frend gives account of the completion of the Christianization of the Mediterranean and its spread beyond the bounds of the Roman Empire. He stated that the church received valuable tax remissions and other privileges. Christians were often favored in the imperial service and the inhabitants of townships could sometimes invoke their devotion to Christianity as a means of winning imperial favor. The Emperors believed, like their pagan predecessors, that material prosperity depended on the observance of the right religion and that the orthodox representatives of the church practiced the right religion.[22] In this new situation, the laity were deprived of their former powers in the inner life of the church, but found scope as its advocates and benefactors. The closeness of the relationship between church and state required the skilled diplomacy of Christian administrators and the influence of these powerful lay officials on church affairs could be great.

At the same time, the persistence of classical education had the effect of training Christian laymen to think in the philosophical terms in which the doctrine of the church was being expressed. As that tradition survived, the laity produced theologians every bit as instructed as the clergy themselves. Within the empire itself, lay influence and example had an enormous effect in promoting a real Christianization of values among the population as a whole. The clergy were the chosen servants of God; the laity were the people.[23]

The clergy were the chosen servants of God; the laity were the people.

The Roman rule was not inclusive of the laity. However, the emperor's position safeguarded that of the laity as a whole. The emperor was a layman, yet no one denied his sacred character or his right to legislate an ecclesiastical matter. He represented the royal priesthood of the people of God; thus, the layman could never be completely ignored.[24] During this period, the ancient world melted into the Middle Ages. The laity played an astonishingly active part in the intellectual and moral life of the church. The succeeding age was less fruitful, but once the pessimism that descended on the western world in the fifth century had lifted, the way was re-opened to full lay discipleship.[25]

The study of the laity, around the eleventh and twelfth centuries, marked a major turning point in European history. The papal (or Gregorian) reform, the crusades, the formation of the Norman states, and many other movements made this a period of dramatic change.[26] Standards of education rose among the higher clergy, Latin literature flourished, and the small circle of humanists expressed their thoughts with a freedom and sophistication unparalleled since the fall of Rome.[27] Laymen were still largely illiterate and based their knowledge on what their clerical contemporaries chose to tell them.

There was no greater fundamental division in medieval life than the division between clergy and laity; especially between the upper clergy, the highly educated, privileged lay leader, and the lay aristocracy. The lay aristocracy were illiterate. They were taught the arts of war and, in a rudimentary way, justice and government. Before the eleventh century, the upper clergy were few in numbers and distinct as a class. After the thirteenth century, especially in the south of Europe, the divergence began to break down rapidly. There had always been lay education in Italy, and many of the great names in Italian thought and literature were laymen, including Dante and others.

The theologians did not lose the view of the church as the community of the faithful, but in the government of the church, and in everyday speech, the church was equivalent to the clerical order. The clergy were the shepherds, laity, and sheep. Even in the church's view, the laity had a role to play. Clergy and laity performed different functions in a world deeply convinced of the importance of function at first sight. It may have been a simple matter for them to agree on their different roles to live and work apart. It became clear that there was nothing in the world more difficult than for ambitious churches and monarchs to agree on the limits of their spheres of activity.[28]

> At the root of many of the movements of the eleventh and twelfth centuries lay a book—the Bible, the Rule of St. Benedict, Justinians Corpus.[29]

This happened in an even more dramatic way in the Renaissance of the fifteenth century. Firstly, the power of the renaissance was conditioned by the number of educated men who could understand its message and appreciate its values. Education was more widespread in the fifteenth century than in the twelfth and affected a cross-section of the lay community. Although the churches retained great power in the universities of Europe, the laity began to play their part in them in the latter middle-ages, especially in Italy. The old framework of clerical learning and lay ignorance no longer corresponded to the facts. The layman's role was changing in the eleventh and twelfth centuries. Men looked at the Bible with new eyes and were led to question the organization of the church and the role of the laity.

The Laity During the Reformation

Gorden Rupp, Professor of Ecclesiastical History at the University of Manchester, provided insight about the laity during the Reformation. On October 31, 1517, Martin Luther nailed ninety-five theses to the door of the castle church at Wittenberg. It was at this time that he joined Saint Frances in Italy, Wycliff in England, Huss in Bohemia, and a multitude of others who felt there were needed changes in the church and that laymen should be recognized. According to Rupp, it was Luther who first expounded the calling of the civil government.[30] It was made in an emergency situation, in which the spiritual authorities had refused self-amendment. Luther appealed to the rulers of Germany on the ground of the common priesthood of all

Christians. Luther's doctrines were compressed in these four points:

1. Before God, all Christians have the same standing, a priesthood in which we enter by baptism and through faith.
2. As a comrade and brother of Christ, each Christian is a priest and needs no mediator, save Christ. He has access to the Word.
3. Each Christian is a priest and has an office of sacrifice; not the mass, but the dedication of himself to the praise and obedience of God, and to bearing the cross.
4. Each Christian has a duty to stand on the gospel, which he has received.

For Martin Luther, there was an important relationship between the Word and the people of God because the gospel creates the church as God through preaching and the sacraments.[31]

In 1537, Bishop Edward Foxe told the English convocation:

> The laypeople do not know the Holy Scripture better than many of us, and the Germans have made the text of the Bible so plain and easy with the Hebrew and the Greek that now many things be better understood without any glasses

> at all than by all the commentaries of the doctors.[32]

During the Reformation, the layman lost his pictures and windows; his bends and primers; his processions, candles, pilgrimages, feasts and fasts. But, he gained his Bible, catechism, prayer book, and hymns. He could share in worship with intelligent awareness. The protestant agenda stated that the laity, especially the young, should be instructed.

The Laity During the Post-Reformation Period

The laity progressed in a contributing role following the Reformation. The Lutheran world, one of the most notable manifestations of the lay spirit, was the expression of the Christian faith. Lutheranism, in the period of orthodoxy, produced a church composed entirely of laymen, which was able to maintain itself through the early period of Pietism up to 1734. In the orthodox churches, whether Lutheran or reformed, the task of the laypeople was to work out the forms and institutions in which the life of these churches was to be carried forward, and to take a responsible share in making the new organization work.[33] The significance of the layman in all the churches in

Europe increased to bring to fruition all that was present in germ form in the Reformation.[34]

In the nineteenth century, Mather, the British layman, stated:

> All too often the layman was thought of merely as an instrument of evangelization. The phrase lay agency, which was frequently on the lips of ecclesiastical reformers in the 1860s, conveys that view clearly and unmistakably.[35]

We have come to see that the task of Christians, whether clerical or lay, is not to do something *for* the church, but to *be* the church.

Three types of church government were common to American life: Episcopal, Congregational, and Presbyterian. In all three, the laity came to a position of considerable influence. The Protestant Episcopal Church is an example of the first type. Although the early canons on the laity rendered concern only for candidates' holy orders, the General Convention of 1871 extended this provision to lay services, including the right, with special license, to deliver and address instructions and exhortations in vacant parishes, congregations, or missions. The number of lay leaders increased from 2,015 in 1900 to 7,750 in 1952 and up to 15,044 in 1960.[36]

The Methodist church is also specially governed in the United States, although its wide use of laymen and its extensive accommodation to the frontier were not always consistent with its policy. By 1850, approximately one-third of the total memberships of American churches were free churches, not including Methodists. The Disciples of Christ (re-designated Christian churches) were also radically lay-centered by their traditions. Thomas and Alexander Campbell, its founders, insisted upon the right of the layman to exhort, teach, and, on occasion, preach. The Presbyterian churches represent a position somewhere in between the two extremes, but has developed a system of lay representation, which extends church government.[37]

We have come to see that the task of Christians, whether clerical or lay, is not to do something for the church, but to be the church.

Massey and McKinney state that most black preachers function in direct relationship to their understanding of their call. The laity vests power in the pastor and officers relating to their functions. The ultimate power in the church, however, is actually in the hands of the church body, and they listen to the leaders of the house. It is true: All of us are wiser than any of us. The laity can detect latent ambitions in one another and, when led by the Spirit, the right decision will be made. We must recognize that the church is a theocracy and not a democracy. When there is a freedom for the set leader to flow under God, a church will flourish.

Empowerment and Entitlement

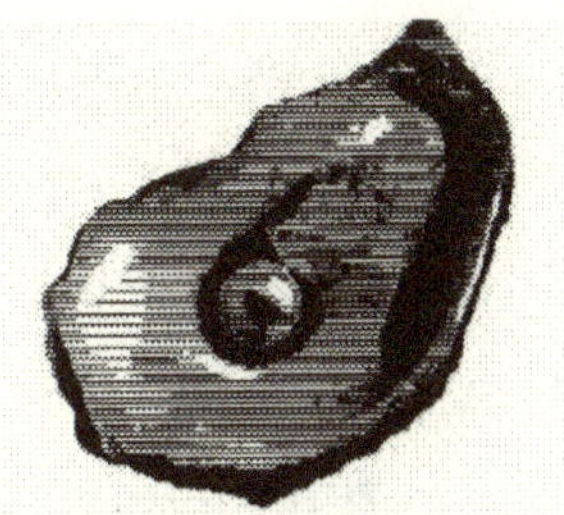

Edward Hamnet states in his book *The Gathered and Scattered*, "For decades, the meaning of church members has been deteriorating."[38] Committed, consecrated, and selfless leaders who not only were committed to God, but also committed to building, developing, and celebrating membership in the local church, bothered most churches. Church membership brought status, belonging, connectedness, and an avenue for proving and improving faithfulness to God and His service.[39] In many churches today, membership is barely a piece of paper. It is easier to join a church than most social organizations, which require payment of dues, attendance, and participation. In social organizations, failure to meet such obligations often results in penalty or dismissal.

People are drawn to places where the vision is clear and expectations are high. People are looking for something that makes a difference because they generally rise to the level of expectations. People are looking for a fertile spiritual environment where they can be empowered and grow.

Once the church receives members, it must consider ways of outlining ministry descriptions that challenge pastors to identify, develop, equip, and empower disciples. The lives and ministry of the disciples are the measuring stick of effectiveness. The pastors must rethink the function of laity.[40]

The pastors must rethink the function of laity.

For example, shared pastoral care can broaden the scope of a church ministry. The growing emotional, physical, and relational needs of our church and community are too great for a limited number of pastoral care givers to handle. Rather than delegate all pastoral care to the ministerial staff and deacons, share the responsibility with the laity. There are pearls in the pews lying in their shells ready to be polished and to have their gifts empowered for kingdom building.

We must change our focus for ministry. For too long, pastors have concentrated on developing and maintaining church programs by increasing membership, budgets, and buildings because these were the symbols of success. However, real ministry includes training people inside and outside the church. It involves participating in life-changing causes and designing paradigms that encourage, enable, equip, and empower Christians to find their place of ministry in the world through exercising their spiritual gifts and calling.

Pastors must move from hands-on ministry to equipping and being leaders of ministry.

We are at a confluence of the changing tides. There is a new social climate. The idea of lay ministry requires pastors to become trainers of leaders. The 1970s and 1980s increased our awareness that there was a place for the ministry of the laity in the body of Christ. The laity has become an active component in the ministry of the congregation. Pastors must move from hands-on ministry to equipping and being leaders of ministry.

Laypersons must understand that because they are empowered through teaching and training, they are not entitled to any special privileges of the church.

Since the Reformation, the pastor has run the operations of a congregation, preached the Word, visited the sick, counseled people, and basically managed the religious organization.[41] The problem is that most pastors were schooled in and model the old paradigm where few thoughts of serious leadership take place. There is a cry from the laity: "I want to experience ministry and exercise my gift, but I need help finding a place. I want to be empowered for ministry." I hear the cry in ministry everywhere I go. This is a noble cry and I believe if Christian ministry is going to be effective, we must listen and take heed.

However, laypersons must understand that because they are empowered through teaching and training, they are not entitled to any special privileges of the church. As a pastor, Christian leader, and trainer, I have seen many people possess a spirit of entitlement because they have been empowered by virtue of their spiritual gift. *"A gift opens the way for the giver and ushers him into the presence of the great" (Proverbs 18:16).* Although people are gifted with certain qualities, they should count it a privilege to serve. They must never use their gifts to manipulate or hold the church hostage as though the church cannot go on if they do not sing, pray, give, or lead a particular ministry. Jesus stated in Matthew: *"And I tell you that you are Peter, and on this rock I will build my church, and the gates of Hades will not overcome it" (Matthew 16:18).*

Laypersons must understand that their gifts are submitted to their church under their pastor's direction.

Laypersons must understand that their gifts are submitted to their church under their pastor's direction. Gifts are not for individual use, they are for building God's kingdom under pastoral leadership. I am aware that when the pastor directs the use of gifts, some may feel they are being held back if they do not use their gifts or talents as they think they should be used. Some may say the Holy Spirit is being quenched or they are being forced to disobey God. Some may leave and go other places, but there is a proper order in God's house.

People with ministry gifts must learn to trust the leading and discernment of their leader, who must determine the order and use of spiritual gifts, and judge the appropriate times and seasons for them in the local body. Gifts must be used in proper order for the church to benefit. When gifts are used without proper order, the glory goes to the person with the gift, and not the giver of the gift. Gifts never rule God's order. God's appointment should always rule the use of gifts.

> *Now you are the body of Christ, and each one of you is a part of it. And in the church God has appointed first of all apostles, second prophets, third teachers, then workers of miracles, also those having gifts of healing, those able to help others, those with gifts of administration, and those speaking in different kinds of tongues. (I Corinthians 12:27–28).*

The gifts that one possess are not your own, but are given to you by the Holy Spirit for service. Your gifts should correspond to the needs of the church. Although you may be empowered with a gift or gifts, you are not entitled to usurp authority over the pastor or anyone else. There are no empire builders or solo performers in God's kingdom.

I believe Nehemiah gave insight on how valuable the laity can be to a congregation when biblical mandates are followed. Nehemiah did nothing until he gathered information and focused his faith on God's ability to work the situation to a point where he could be useful to the Lord. He was certain to never betray the trust of those who were over him, nor those for whom he had the responsibility of leading. When Nehemiah received the news that Jerusalem was in ruins, it touched him deeply, but before acting, he first sought the Lord's face and submitted the matter in prayer. Once he felt secure in his prayers, he waited for the Lord to help him present the matter to the king as a petition (Nehemiah 1). He showed a great sense of respect for his king, not wanting to do more than he could handle, asking for no more than he needed, and taking no more time than was necessary to get the job done.

Empowerment and entitlement are more than titles.

Nehemiah used the empowerment given to him by King Artaxerxes to create a system. The projected wall was divided into manageable sections with clearly defined tasks (Nehemiah 3–5). Some were stationed as watchmen, others as soldiers, and others provided food. Workers hauled off debris as it accumulated. Everyone understood his part, and the wall went up. Nehemiah was extremely respectful. When the city of Jerusalem was finally built, he did not take spiritual matters into his own hands. Instead, he called for Ezra, the teaching priest, and assisted this man of God in conducting the worship and information session that was essential to bringing the people into spiritual unity. Nehemiah was not concerned about a title.

Empowerment and entitlement are more than titles. There are inherent dangers in being caught up on titles. Some Christians would be better off if they were never given titles such as deacon, trustee, chairman, or president. It seems that titles are connected with power and people attempt to usurp authority over others, including the God-set leader.

Power in leadership is the acceptance of a life of dependence expressed in human weakness, with a corresponding confidence in the power of Christ. No person can jump into a place of spiritual leadership because of a title. I have seen many good people who seemingly accepted the church's vision and supported every ministry until they were placed in a position of leadership. Titles can be dangerous when appointed to people who do not love God, respect leadership, and have a servant spirit.

Titles can be dangerous when appointed to people who do not love God, respect leadership, and have a servant spirit.

For example, I have met many preachers who will state their titles before stating their names. I caution my sons and daughters in ministry to be mindful of exploiting a title. Whenever you are asked to give your name, give your name, e.g., "My name is John

Walker." I should state the name my mother gave me, not Reverend or Doctor, simply John Walker. One should never reverence himself. I have known many preachers to get upset when someone failed to call them Bishop, Reverend, or Doctor. It is sad when we are more concerned about our titles than we are about the work of ministry.[42]

The missing component in our churches is not leaders, but disciples.

Bishop Larry Trotter stated in a sermon that titles are dangerous because some folks become arrogant and puffed up.[43] I am convinced that the New Testament never told us to make leaders and give them titles, but rather, to make disciples of men. The missing component in our churches is not leaders, but disciples. I contend that if we make disciples, leadership will become like cream—it will rise to the top.

Ministry is dead unless it has been empowered by the Holy Spirit. People join the church and commit to an anointed leader. They want to be empowered by the leader's God-given vision. When people are connected to their leader, they prosper and become fruitful. Our church expects people to invest themselves in serving Jesus by serving people. Isolation and individualism are a part of the problem, not part of the solution. We must understand that relationships are essential to health and maturity.

One key question we must raise regarding empowerment and entitlement is: Where does servant leadership fit in? We must not integrate the issue of power with servant leaders. Because servant leadership can take on many forms, serving people may appear as having power over them. The entire issue of empowerment begins with the discussion of power and entitlement. First, I must admit that as a leader, I have legitimate, positional power. Secondly, I must admit that as a sinner, I can easily deceive myself, believing

We must not integrate the issue of power with servant leaders. Because servant leadership can take on many forms, serving people may appear as having power over them.

that empowerment means I am entitled to some special privilege because I have been chosen and selected by the leaders to serve. Thirdly, I must pray that God will create in me a genuine desire to please Him and serve others.

It is scary to think that twelve men could be in the company of Jesus day after day, listen to His leadership, watch His ways, and, yet, not get it. It is even more frightening that people can sit under a liberating word week after week and die in their seats because they are too mean and prideful to change their ways and walk in the Word.

In Luke 9:46, an argument started among the disciples as to which of them would be the greatest in the kingdom. Jesus' followers grew up in a culture that understood only one politic: POWER—the power of kings and armies, the power of the religious community pronouncing or denying God's approval, the power of family, village, and tribal tradition ruling people to mindless conformity or "the way we do things." The concept of power was hardwired into the very fiber of their souls. They were sensitized to locating sources of such power, submitting to them or using them to their advantage. They were used to exercising power if in a position to do so. The disciples were empowered, but the temptation of entitlement was lurking deep within. It was natural for them to decide who was the most faithful and genuine; who would run things when Jesus was absent; who would prevail when decisions were to be made; who was in charge. These debates seemed to happen when they preoccupied themselves with rights, privileges, and entitlement.

Not much has changed in our churches. Too often we are hindered in our relationships because we are more concerned with our agenda than with God's agenda; with our way than with God's way; with our dreams than with God's vision. This politic over which there was so much misunderstanding is one of the great divisions among the saints of God today. Church members still seek to dominate, intimidate, control, or win people over by serving them.

The disciples had enough of serving the Romans, the religious establishment, and the rich. Yet, the Son of God was asking them to adopt a servanthood perspective for a new and different reason. They thought Jesus was their chance to break out, to become the power brokers instead of being power-broken by the Holy Spirit.

The disciples should have had a kingdom mindset and been an extension of the message of Christ. In order for a ministry to achieve its mission, and for a church to grow, membership must fill certain roles. The laity must not lie dormant in the pew, content with being saved, with no vision of moving beyond salvation into kingdom living. In his book, *Sin in the House*, Dr. George O. McCalep, Jr., states that one of the ten crucial hindrances to church growth is that too many folks are stuck on salvation and will not move any further.[44] There must be some pearls who understand their value to the kingdom. A church vision is beyond a catchy phrase, cute slogan, or fancy logo. People who see how their contribution connects to the whole body of Christ fulfill visions.

People who see how their contribution connects to the whole body of Christ fulfill visions.

There must be some *influencers, contributors,* and *managers* in the body for a ministry to achieve its mission. *Influencers* get excited about the vision.

They are quick to share the reasons why everyone needs to buy into the vision. Influencers not only get people excited, but help the doubters and naysayers believe that if they work together, they can accomplish a mission bigger than they could individually. Influencers inspire an organization.

Contributors are people who, if properly positioned, get the work done and have the skills to deliver ministry so that lives are touched and transformed.[45] Churches are hindered in moving to another level because too many people refuse to give up some position in order for those who can get the job done to accomplish the task. Many would rather hinder the church than give up a position they hold ineffectively. Contributors give all of themselves—time, talent, and financial resources.

Churches are hindered in moving to another level because too many people refuse to give up some position in order for those who can get the job done to accomplish the task.

Managers are the missing persons in most ministries, but they have been designed by God to provide what contributors need to succeed. Managers know the needs and desires of contributors, but their ministry is to coordinate, plan, and troubleshoot. Managers do not do the work of ministry, but uphold those who do. They are not intimidated by anyone else's gift. Day in and day out, they patiently keep the membership encouraged and resourced.

Managers do not do the work of ministry, but uphold those who do.

The early church spread not only by the preaching of those few who were gifted as preachers and evangelists, but also through the quiet and faithful witness of ordinary Christians to their pagan neighbors. Paul wrote to the young Thessalonian church:

> *The Lord's message rang out from you not only in Macedonia and Achaia—your faith in God has become known everywhere (1 Thessalonians 1:8).*

The mobilization of the church, including the clergy and laity, must be repeated for this millennium. This means we must focus more intently on discipleship. It means we must repent of our compromises and our failure to demonstrate the transforming power and love of Christ in our lives, and learn afresh what it means to be salt and light in a dark, decaying world. It also means that we encourage the discovery and development of the spiritual gifts we see in other folk.

A true pearl wrestles with what John Ortberg calls the disciples' dilemma: sit at His feet or serve in His name.[46] True pearls seize the day, devote themselves to kingdom work, and do not rest in the pew as benchwarmers. In I Corinthians 15:58, Paul states:

> *Therefore, my dear brothers, stand firm. Let nothing move you. Always give yourselves fully to the work of the Lord, because you know that your labor in the Lord is not in vain.*

The mobilization of the church, including the clergy and laity, must be repeated for this millennium. This means we must focus more intently on discipleship.

As a Christian, my desire is to discover the deepest passions that God hardwired into me. I want to develop whatever gifts I have to the fullest. When I sit at Christ's feet I am empowered to serve in His name. One cannot serve in His name until he/she has sat at His feet. Abiding is what Jesus asked us to do. Taking up a cross is not an easy thing. Before you can be used by God and placed on display to shine as a pearl, you must take up a cross. Remember that He is Lord of the cross. Jesus said, *"Abide in me, and I in you" (John 15:4 KJV).* No branch can bear fruit by itself, it must abide. Neither can you bear fruit by yourself, you must abide.[47] I am convinced that laity must abide under the cover of leadership in order to produce fruit.

The word *abide* means "to remain, dwell, or be deeply rooted." Too often we abide as long as we have our way. Whenever it is time to change our positions or rotate us for the betterment of the kingdom, our leader becomes our public enemy number one. It is a sad day in the church when membership begins to play games in the house of God. We teach people to join a church rather than the vision of the leader. It is assumed that belonging to a church will provide people a meaningful life. Any church that encourages membership only will not experience true discipleship. We can become more concerned with keeping people rather than drawing people. What is so amazing is that Jesus never told us to make members. He said to make disciples. Nowhere is it written that people should join a church just to receive a membership.

Any church that encourages membership only will not experience true discipleship.

We must revisit the first century church where believers were joined to the message of the leaders and not of a board or committee. There is an ongoing power struggle in many churches between pulpits, key persons, boards, and laypersons who seek to control and manipulate congregations in ways that please themselves. The spirit of rebellion is strong in any church where tradition-minded people are in control.

In churches where the pastor is not recognized as the overseer of the house, the deacons become demons, trustees become trifling, church conferences become church confrontations, and the Sunday worship becomes a place where people with cold hearts give other people the cold shoulder. Pastors will turn the pulpit into a battleground rather than fill the pews with pearls. The Pastor's study becomes a place of plotting rather than prayer.[48] If membership is to be equipped for ministry, we must cultivate the oyster and raise up the priceless pearls so that God may receive the glory.

Empowerment is about the right people being in the right place for the right reasons.

Pastors must remember that more people become committed when they are serving in ministries that allow them to operate using their gifts and calling. A Christ-centered ministry makes every effort to discover a person's unique gifts and calling. A Christ-centered ministry encourages people to serve where God has equipped them to do so. A ministry mindset starts with the assumption that a local church has all the gifted people it needs to accomplish the ministries God intends it to have right now. Empowerment is about the right people being in the right place for the right reasons. When this happens, the message suggests to your church, your neighborhood, and the world that Christ lives in and through every person. When God's people live out their discipleship in ways that proclaim the Savior, lives are changed.

For attaining wisdom and discipline; for understanding words of insight; for acquiring a disciplined and prudent life, doing what is right and just and fair; for giving prudence to the simple, knowledge and discretion to the young—let the wise listen and add to their learning, and let the discerning get guidance (Proverbs 1:2–5).

The Polishing of a Pearl

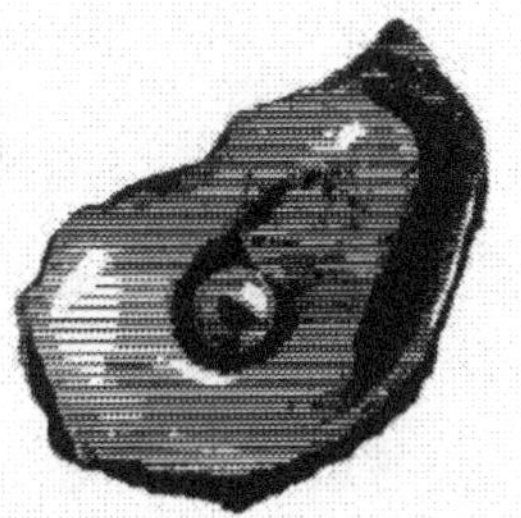

One of the most important activities of the church is leadership development. To address the problem of undefined leadership, I have developed a **Laity Leadership Training** program to recruit and equip leaders on an ongoing basis. The remainder of this book describes the program and gives step-by-step instructions for implementing it in your church.

Leadership training is a method of achieving church organizational goals. McDonough points out that without trained leaders, an endeavor has two strikes against it before it starts. The quality of work that a person performs is directly linked to his preparation for the task. Laity leadership training prepares lay members of a local congregation to serve as leaders. Without trained leadership, organizations will have great difficulty becoming successful. Trained leadership will ensure that the organization has competent leaders and workers for ministry. Training improves organizational efficiency, leader competency, and ministry effectiveness.

Identifying Potential Leaders for the Church

Training improves organizational efficiency, leader competency, and ministry effectiveness.

The first step in recruiting people for leadership training is to determine the general characteristics of Christian leaders. After the general leadership characteristics are defined, it is necessary for the pastor of the church to identify laypersons who will benefit from the training. This plan of enlistment depends upon the Lord's help and leadership. Without the guidance of the Holy Spirit, there is no guarantee of success. One must pray continually throughout the endeavor of enlisting leaders (1 Thessalonians 5:17).

Selection Criteria #1: Leaders Should Be Spiritual

This quality is imperative for work in the cause of Christ. I believe that morality should be included in spirituality. Low morality will not sustain leadership. Without a moral life, the influence of leadership vanishes. The person chosen for this training should possess not only a high level of morality, but also must have encountered Jesus Christ as Lord and Savior.

No man can satisfactorily serve, as a channel of God's message if he does not have the inner resources and deep personal experience with Christ to interpret that message to others. Without these resources and this experience, he would be like a well without water and clouds without rain. Spirituality, therefore, is the primary prerequisite to leadership within the church.

You will find very little emphasis placed on leadership skills by present day writers or in the twentieth century writings from Justin Martyr through Julian of Norwich. What you will find, however, are exhortations for all Christians to pursue holiness, renounce self-centeredness, endure suffering, and pray. The focus is placed less on skills and more on character, for if one's spiritual character is developed, the pearl of leadership will evolve.

Selection Criteria #2: Leaders Should Be Educable

Laity in training should possess the native capacities necessary to become a leader. Although their educational background may be limited, people may be considered potential church leaders if they can learn quickly, make sound judgments, and display an interest in assuming additional responsibility. The importance of these qualities cannot be over emphasized since they are needed in all areas of life.

Selection Criteria #3: Leaders Should Be Cooperative

While many people are dismissed from their jobs in the secular world because they lack knowledge or technical competence, just as many are dismissed because they do not have the social understanding and ability to get along with others. The person selected for leadership training should be able to get along with other potential leaders and have a spirit of cooperation. Otherwise, major problems within the ranks of leadership could arise.

Selection Criteria #4: Leaders Should Possess a Spirit of Dedication

This quality may be defined as the act of committing oneself to a program and to those who are part of the program. When we dedicate ourselves to God, we set ourselves apart for God's work. We commit ourselves to the plan that God has designed. If people are connected with a particular group, they should exert every effort to influence the development of the group's program.

Dedicated people are usually responsible and loyal. Being responsible assures that the individual will work to complete the task according to plan despite all obstacles. Loyalty demands that he accept the program as his, and is true to the program until the most minute detail is executed. These qualities are necessary because without responsibility and loyalty, the lines of communication dissolve.

When we dedicate ourselves to God, we set ourselves apart for God's work. We commit ourselves to the plan that God has designed.

All leaders need limited assistance. However, a person who requires constant guidance, is indifferent to responsibilities, or is deliberately unfaithful to the training should not be selected to serve, except in positions of limited responsibility. He should not be placed in a key leadership position until he is prepared to assume a full share of the workload in a spirit of trust and dedication.

Selection Criteria #5: Leaders Should Display Genuine Enthusiasm

Enthusiasm is contagious. It influences others to become involved. Enthusiasm is a quality of mind, characterizing a person who enjoys serving. People enjoy doing things that give them a sense of achievement. Enthusiasm manifests itself in overt ways, including gestures, voice inflection, facial expressions, and head movements.

The first step in developing enthusiasm is working within one's calling. The second step is demonstrating a feeling of enjoyment in ways that are perceptible to others. Although one may be well educated and have previous work experience, if he lacks enthusiasm, it will be exceedingly difficult for him to function effectively in an important leadership position.

Equipping Leaders

People who have the above qualities are potential leaders. Once your potential leaders are selected, the next step is to invite them to cross over social, economic and educational backgrounds, titles, offices and ministries, and join a Laity Leadership Training program, which will prepare them to answer their call to leadership and ministry.

Equipping is a better concept than training because it more accurately describes the leadership training process. Training is a part of the equipping process that prepares a person for leadership. Training is generally focused on specific jobs or tasks. For example, a person is trained to use a company machine or to answer a phone in a particular way.

According to John Maxwell, "Equipping is like an unskilled person scaling a tall mountain peak." His preparation is a process. He needs to be outfitted with equipment, such as cold weather clothing, ropes, picks, and spikes; and he needs to be trained in the use of that equipment. A mountain climber's preparation, however, involves much more than having the correct equipment and knowing how to use it. The person must be conditioned physically for the difficult climb. He must be trained to be a part of a team. Most importantly, he must be taught to think like a mountain climber. He needs to be able to look at a peak and determine how it may best be conquered. Without going through the complete equipping process, he may find himself stranded on the side of a mountain freezing to death.

Equipping the laity for leadership is similar. Equipping, like nurturing, is an ongoing process. One cannot equip a person in a few hours or in a day. Equipping must flow from the equipper's theology of ministry and must be tailored to each church.

Pastors/teachers must be advisors who own the vision of the church and can communicate it to others. They must become equippers who can impart the vision, evaluate the potential leaders, provide the tools they need, and mentor them along the way. Pastors/teachers also instill the desire to work. They are able to lead, teach, and assess the progress of the people being equipped.

Equipping must flow from the equipper's theology of ministry and must be tailored to each church.

Pastor's Questionnaire

Effective equipping begins with asking questions. If certain questions are avoided, people may miss the crucial significance of the equipping process. The Laity Leadership Training program uses a Pastor's Questionnaire to clarify the mission of the church and the leader's theology of ministry. These questions address the equipping process from the pastor's perspective. The pastor must set the tone for the equipping process, including his own theology of ministry.

The questionnaire has two parts. Part I addresses the mission of the church. Part II focuses on the pastor's theology. Examples of the questions follow. I have provided the reason for each question to help you understand the process. These explanations would not appear on the actual questionnaire.

Laity Leadership Training
Pastor's Questionnaire
Part I: The Mission of the Church

1. What is the mission statement of the church?

The development of leaders in an organization must begin with a review of the ministry's purpose because equipping or training should contribute to the fulfillment of the that purpose.

2. What is the primary need of the ministry?

This question connects the general mission with specific needs.

3. What areas within the ministry have the greatest growth potential?

This question stimulates people to consider an offensive rather than defensive posture so the ministry is positioned to meet the future.

4. Do those potential growth areas have the needed leaders to accomplish the tasks?

Lay leaders are required to meet the future head on. If the laity is not equipped, growth potential will never move from potential to reality. If these leaders do not presently exist, they must be identified, developed, and equipped for ministry. The clergy cannot carry out the full ministry of the church alone.

Part II: The Theology of the Pastor/Teacher

1. Am I willing to pour my life into others?

Giving to others is a way of life for effective leaders. The best contribution of pastoral leaders is to train others to become leaders in their own areas of expertise by helping them to discover their spiritual gifts, and by showing them how to actualize their new-found skills in the work of the kingdom. Pastors know that development of their people is more important than the development of their own status. Equipping involves sacrifice.

2. Am I committed to an equipping ministry?

Equipping requires commitment. It takes time and effort on the part of a pastor. It may be quicker and easier for a pastor to do the work himself rather than teach other people, but doing it himself is a short-term solution. The long, hard road of equipping others pays off in the long run, and it requires commitment from everyone in the church.

3. Am I effective in the areas in which my leaders need to be equipped?

This is a difficult question that requires an honest answer. The pastor/teacher must first be equipped, and then be willing to equip the saints. If the answer is no, the pastor must either take the time to become equipped or locate someone inside or outside the church who is effective in those areas and can administer some of the training.

Laity Leadership Training Course

The Laity Leadership Training course is designed with the latitude to be tailored to your ministry. I understand that each church is different and each ministry may have a different leadership model. Therefore, the content and length of your course may vary from what is shown here. However, I believe there are some things that are critical to equipping the laity and germane to an effective leadership course. I suggest that your course includes the following topics:

1. The Pastor's Theology of Ministry
2. The Prerequisite of Christian Leadership
3. The Preparation of Leadership
4. The Practice of Leadership
5. Deacons' Ministry Training
   (Reference: *A Fresh Look at New Testament Leader*)
6. The Vision of Leadership

The remainder of this chapter describes the components of the Laity Leadership Training course. The information presented here is not intended to be a complete course that is ready to be taught. It will be necessary for you to create a course that meets the unique needs of your ministry. The information I am providing will guide you through that process. Following these guidelines will give you the benefit of a proven structure and the insight I have gained from successfully implementing the Laity Leadership Training program.

When creating your course, keep in mind that the material must be simple enough to understand, yet challenging enough to movitvate the participants to learn. The material should stimulate attention, be relevant to the subject, build confidence, and create a satisfying experience for each participant.

The appendices of this book contain administrative tools to assist you in conducting the course, including a letter to the participants, an attendance log, a training manual for participants, a course evaluation, and a graduate certificate. Please note that each participant should receive a printed training manual.

The course can be taught on a regularly scheduled weeknight. The length will depend on your selected content. The course, as decribed here, is presented in twelve weeks.

Course Orientation

The course begins with orienting the participants to the training program and working with each other. It is important that everyone understands the program goals, expectations, and requirements. In addition to the course content, it is necessary to begin team building immediately. The following will guide you throught the orientation.

Introductions: Know Who Is Who

Most of the people from the same church will already know each other, but having an opportunity to introduce themselves to the class establishes cohesion and fosters inclusion.

Expectations: Know What Is Expected

Participants need to know the requirements and expectations regarding:

- Attendance
- Participation
- Supplies (e.g., Bibles, pens, note pads, etc.)

Objectives: Understand the Goals and Obligations of the Program

The objective of the Laity Leadership Training program is to prepare ministry leaders for the twenty-first century. The training includes leadership principles and understanding the vision of the church. People need clear objectives set before them at the start of the program. A set of goals and objectives becomes a map for the laity to follow in order to grow.

Relevance: Identify with the Program

Participants need to understand how this training is relevant to your church. Help them see that the Laity Leadership Training program is a means of:

- fulfilling God's purpose for your church.
- meeting the primary need of the church.
- expanding the ministry.
- positioning the ministry to meet future needs.

Understanding the relevance of the training enables the participants to identify with the program. It also fosters a sense of inclusion.

Course Introduction

The introductory lesson gives the potential leaders a clearly defined description of the course. The lesson objective is for the participants to understand that one of the primary goals of the Laity Leadership Training course is to provide the pastor, church, and ministries with Christian leaders who are qualified to meet the needs of a growing membership and understand the pastor's theology of ministry. They should also learn what is required of each participant in terms of attendance, materials, participation requirements, and selection processes.

It is necessary for the membership to know the pastor's role in the life of the church. This unit allows the potential leader to hear firsthand from the pastor the calling that God has placed on his/her life. Also, it is important and beneficial for the potential leaders to realize that the call on their lives can drive them, unlike any material, financial, or superficial reward.

What is Laity?

There is a need for each person to know his value to a ministry. This begins by understanding the meaning and value of laity, which was discussed in more detail in Chapter 1, "The Making of a Pearl." The laity must have vision and be able to run with it. Habakkuk 2:2 says, *"Then the Lord replied: 'Write down the revelation and make it plain on tablets so that a herald may run with it.'"*

They must see their leader having a clear sense of a desired outcome and the ability to communicate that vision to others. The laity must avoid wrong paradigms such as:

- "We pay them to do all the work."
- "I am not qualified to do it."

- "The job is being done well enough now. There is no point in my trying to do it and messing it up."
- "I can't be bothered. I'm too busy."

The Pastor's Theology of Ministry

It is helpful for the pastor to articulate his/her theology at this point. I will share my theology as an example.

My theology of ministry is rooted in strong spiritual convictions and biblical principles regarding:

- A call to the ministry
- The pastor's role in assisting the local assembly in fulfilling the Great Commission
- The church's purpose and corresponding functions
- Key Christian concepts
- The role of laity in the life of the church

I believe God called me to preach His gospel by His sovereign grace. The authority of this call is the prerogative of Christ alone, for He calls whomever He wills. He told His disciples, *"You did not choose me, but I chose you and appointed you to go and bear fruit—fruit that will last" (John 15:16).* We read in Mark 3:13–14 that Christ called whomever He wanted.

Even of Paul, the Lord said, *"Go! This man is my chosen instrument to carry my name before the Gentiles and their kings and before the people of Israel" (Acts 9:15).* Before I was born, God knew that He would call me into the gospel ministry. God, in the midst of His general call, dealt with me individually. My call was personal. He burdened my heart and impressed upon me the necessity of preaching the gospel. This burden was the Holy Spirit guiding my thoughts into a certain and definite conviction as to God's will for my life.

I knew there was a general call to salvation for everyone. At the moment of belief, Jesus becomes Savior. He forgives all sin and removes them *"as far as the east is from the west" (Psalms 103:12).* When one trusts Christ, the salvation he receives is for eternity. By faith he is born again and that faith is from above. One's spiritual birth makes him a child of God. The Christian's life is an everlasting life because he has an eternal salvation. There is nothing fleeting or temporary about the soul salvation that Jesus gives. God is the keeper (John 10:28). Man cannot save himself. Man cannot keep himself. God can and does both, through Jesus Christ.

There is a process to spiritual maturity that begins with spiritual birth. The conversion experience is not the end of one's walk with God; it is the beginning. It is the first step, not the last. Just as an infant has to grow, a new Christian is also expected to grow. Growth must begin in the Christian through conversion. The preaching of the gospel is the means of this conversion experience. *"God was pleased through the foolishness of what was preached to save those who believe" (1 Corinthians 1:21).* As a pastor, I must preach for *"how can they hear without someone preaching to them?" (Romans 10:14).*

The pastor/preacher is to deliver the Word of God. I have no message, no story, and no power apart from a position of leadership. The excellency of the power of proclamation is of God and not of us. Believers do not attend worship service week after week to hear the pastor's opinion or thoughts. They come to hear the Word of God. The gospel message must come from God and move to Christ, being led by the Holy Spirit to a resting place in the believer's heart. The message must declare the gospel in the language and culture of the people in such a way that it is therapeutic, receivable, and liberating.

Laity must perceive that the Spirit of the Lord is upon the preacher.

A pastor must have congregational sensitivity. Jesus was a master at this skill. When He talked to tax collectors, He used their jargon. When He talked to fishermen, He adapted His message to them. The pastor/preacher needs to know the sheep to whom he preaches if he is to speak a relevant, understandable word in their ears that they might hear. He may need to go down to the market places or the jails, wherever the people gather, so he can listen to their conversations, their hurts, and their values, and then speak the Word boldly and profoundly.

Laity must perceive that the Spirit of the Lord is upon the preacher. They must believe that he has been anointed to preach the gospel to the poor, heal the brokenhearted, preach deliverance to the captives, recover sight to the blind, give liberty to the oppressed, and proclaim the acceptable year of the Lord (Luke 4:18, 19). My theology, as it relates to preaching, recognizes that it is God who anoints by His Holy Spirit.

There are many contributing factors to Christian growth. In order for one to grow, there must be a complete yielding to the Master. I believe that Christian growth comes through not only preaching, but also through the teaching of the gospel. When Christians are taught the Word of God, growth is inevitable. I see myself in the role of a servant sharing the Word with God's sheep. I am not the ultimate authority with all earthy and heavenly answers. I must humbly share and present the eternal truths of the Bible. God has given the church the Great Commission. The pastor/teacher must first be equipped, and then be willing to equip the saints for the work of ministry. Just as strong bodies result from years of rigorous exercise and rugged control, Christian maturity is the result of long years of walking with God in deep devotion and sacrificial

The pastor/ teacher must first be equipped, and then be willing to equip the saints for the work of ministry.

discipleship. Unfortunately, Christians occasionally become complacent in the church. Many have been Christians for years, but have not grown spiritually.

The pastor is expected to shepherd the sheep by feeding them the Word of God. In the Afro-centric culture, the pastor has to be diverse enough in his delivery to reach both the typical person on the street and the academic scholar. He must view his role as a teaching elder as he proclaims the Word of God.

Although he is democratically elected as pastor by a majority vote of the church, theologically he has been sent by God. *"Then I will give you shepherds after my own heart, who will lead you with knowledge and understanding" (Jeremiah 3:15)*. He does not belong to the people, although he serves them day and night. He belongs to God who made him and sent him. He is not for show or style, but a servant ready for service; not to be ministered unto, but to minister. He is, because God is. He can do, because God is doing. He must know who he is, whose he is, and why he is.

The Holy Spirit has equipped the church with potential leaders to do the ministry of the church. The role of the pastor is to *discover, enlist,* and *utilize* the resources that are available. It is the pastor's responsibility to teach and equip the flock, but the church belongs to Christ.

The church is God's divine institution. It is through the church that people have experienced unconditional positive regard. The church has a holy mission and a sacred message. It is not just another earthly organization, and is more like an organism than an organization. It is alive. Jesus said, *"And on this rock I will build my church..." (Matthew 16:18)*. The church has a mission—both mighty and eternal. The Great Commission was given to the church by the Master.

The Holy Spirit has equipped the church with potential leaders to do the ministry of the church. The role of the pastor is to discover, enlist, and utilise the resources that are available.

That is why I look upon baptism as a church ordinance. The other ordinance is the Lord's Supper. This ordinance portrays Jesus in his meaningful mission of human redemption. Knowing human frailty and the tendency to forget, Jesus gave this meaningful picture of Himself. It shows how He wants to be remembered.

There are prerequisites for observing the ordinances. In the New Testament, baptism was administered to those who believed. Regarding the Lord's Supper, the Bible says, *"This cup is the new covenant in my blood; do this, whenever you drink it, in remembrance of me" (1 Corinthians 11:25).* Regarding qualifications for one's eligibility to partake of the Lord's Supper, we attempt to limit those who partake of the Lord's Supper to those who are members of the church. All denominations and all churches of those who partake must meet certain requirements, and rightly so.

Every believer is a priest... Everyone has direct access to God through Christ.

Most churches follow the teaching that baptism by immersion is a prerequisite for partaking of the Lord's Supper. As far as we can learn from the Scriptures, those who partook were always baptized believers. By logic, the ordinances should come in that order. Baptism must come first, followed by the Lord's Supper. The point of theological difference has come when we require baptism to be by immersion of the believer on church authority, by a proper administrator, and for the scriptural purpose.

Every believer is a priest. The priesthood of the believer is significant. Approaches to God are not made through human ministers or earthly priests. Everyone has direct access to God through Christ. Therefore, everyone has a right to express feelings concerning the Lord's leading in their lives.

The church is a place for Christian fellowship where Christians feel deep love and experience fellowship with one another. *"We know that we have passed from death to life, because we love our brothers" (1 John 3:14).* The church is a family. Historically, the church and family have provided that cooperation.

African-American churches developed out of the deprivation and oppression experienced by the slaves. The church existed as a support system for the oppressed at society's breakpoints. Without question, the worst breakpoint in this "slavocracy" was the separation of family members. Mothers, fathers, sons, and daughters were consistently sold at the master's whims. The church evolved as a new family for those who were continually being uprooted from their original families.[49] The church is an extended family that serves as a sanctuary for those families that are broken and hurting. Therefore, the church must develop ways to build bridges into the community so it can encounter the problems that continue to erode the family's effectiveness. However, to do this, the church must first rethink its core theology—ecclesiology.

For example, theological reflection can be done through pastoral visitation and care in the workplace. Giving attention to today's workplace issues such as stress, downsizing, diversity training, cultural sensitivity, changing management, financial struggles, and the impact of technology, provides insights that can can help churches. These insights enable the church to:

- assess workers' gifts and motivation.
- lead believers to apply biblical truths to their daily lives.
- inform its teaching, preaching, meeting agendas, ministry plans, and outreach/evangelism strategies.

We must also be open to innovative types of ministries. One of the major challenges Christians face in the twenty-first century is to make the invisible church visible in our secular culture. For decades,

Christian leaders have sought to build up the body of Christ by developing institutions to be salt, light, and leaven in the community in which the church was located. These efforts have succeeded at constructing buildings and increasing membership in those institutions, but the lives of the members are not unlike those in the un-churched population. We must not only improve the quality of our Christian living, we must also take it outside the walls of the institutional church. After all, those outside the church need the message of Christ that the church was created to share.

The church will only be as strong as the families within it because the families make up the laity, and the laity are the pearls in the pews.

The church is a paradigm through which the goods and resources can be shared to care for the needy. The attitude of the church should be one that produces involvement in education, feeding the hungry, and working with the homeless. The church will only be as strong as the families within it because the families make up the laity, and the laity are the *pearls in the pews*.

Families need to extend themselves beyond brokenness for the purpose of finding intimacy within a church environment. Oppressed and dysfunctional families should be able to come to the church in all their brokenness and find a place where surrogate mothers and fathers, brothers and sisters, uncles and aunts are willing to adopt them into their fold. The church should provide single parents, of either sex, role models of the opposite sex to whom children can relate. The church should be a place where youngsters who have known only violence can receive love, and where senior citizens can have faces and voices instead of being talked about as if they were faceless numbers. The family has so influenced the church that it is now a home for the homeless.

I must teach people in my place of ministry to use what God has given to each member to carry out the mission of the church.

My theological assumption rests with the belief that God, the Creator, is also the parent of humankind. God is the one who indeed is, as we so often preach, a mother to the motherless and a father to the fatherless. God is a friend who is closer than a brother. As a parent, God is in relationship with us, not as some abstract absent premise, but as a living, breathing, caring friend who is only a prayer away. Yet, God is also the Creator, and because we are His creation, only God alone knows how to "fix us."

As a Christian leader, I understand that I must teach people in my place of ministry to use what God has given to each member to carry out the mission of the church. Therefore, I believe in an individual approach to ministry, which is centered on people.

Members are motivated for service because the service (ministry) opportunities are focused around their interests and needs. In this view of ministry, the church exists to provide for the needs of the people, rather than the people for the needs of the church. An individual approach to ministry seeks to identify the special gifts, skills, experiences, background, and concerns of the members to match them with appropriate ministry positions in the church. If there are none that seem to fit, a new ministry is created. The membership is the church's most valuable commodity. Membership is the church and the work of the church should be accomplished through the members of the church.

The question yet remains: Is the pastor called to lead or to follow where the fold wants him to go? Is he/she free to lead the sheep, the flock of God, over which the Holy Ghost places overseers? If the congregation is in tune with the Holy Spirit, one would know that the church is not a democracy, but a theocracy—God ruled and Spirit-led in precepts, concepts, and practice. The local church was ordained by Christ when He deliberately gave the keys to the pastors, represented by the apostle Peter and the remaining eleven, before He left the earth (Matthew16:13–20; 28:19; Mark 16). This key given to the pastor is not ruled by deacons' boards or pillar saints. The keys to the kingdom are committed to the pastor.[50]

This does not rule out lay parishioners participating in decision-making and feeling ownership of programs and projects that perpetuate the gospel, visitation to the sick, and relief of human ignorance and suffering. The Holy Spirit places the pastor to train, teach, and direct the church in how to fulfil its mission.[51]

The Prerequisite of Leadership (Being a Leader)

Being a leader has to do with one's mindset. The keys to being an effective leader lie in understanding the corporate nature and vision of the local church, and learning to take spiritual direction from the pastor and other leaders before striking out on one's own understanding. The laity cannot receive the vision for the church when the pastor acquiesces so that his/her job is secure. Only when the pastor comes forth with the God-breathed Word, will the congregation consent to march forward.

This has nothing to do with peoples' ability or inability to perceive what the Lord is doing. Rather, it has to do with the orderliness of the church structure. God gave the earth. There is no tension created when the Lord speaks to the pastor, and then the pastor speaks to the people. This does not preclude that lay people have no mind.[52] The pastor and the people must have the mind of Christ. The mind of Christ is the attitude of a servant pleasing the Master, Christ. All Christians, therefore, are under obligation to honor their Master in all things, including the work of the church.

The Preparation of Leadership (Becoming a Leader)

Parishioners become leaders through a process of God's anointing and being equipped for leadership by the pastor. When a congregation is properly trained, there is never a need for a business meeting of the congregation, but rather a clear vision-casting gathering where ministry is uplifted and the people of God vote *yes* to the will of the Lord and *no* to the evil one and his emissaries who keep the church off target. Only when lay members are trained can they be expected to lead in the right way. In order for them to function in the kind of leadership roles that our Lord intended for His church, the training and direction for ministry in the local church must come from the God-anointed pastor/teacher who the Holy Spirit has seen fit to place over the local congregation.[53]

The Practice of Leadership (Doing as a Leader)

God has equipped the pastor to know better than anyone within the congregation whether or not someone is suitable for leadership. The work of the church requires a team spirit. When any one of the team members is no longer loyal to the pastor, he/she should be excused from participation as a group leader within the church.

There are no exceptions to the biblical mandate for qualified leadership within the church. Laity must support their pastor, commending him/her and thanking God for the pastoral leadership in the one the Holy Spirit has appointed to feed and lead the flock. Congregations should ease pastoral burdens by quelling any subversive action brought into their midst by people who want to lead, but are not equipped to either lead or follow cooperatively.

A congregation should give the pastor unlimited backing on the subject of training and retaining leaders. The pastor should have the option of limiting the tenure of lay leaders who:

- are against the vision.
- destroy unity.
- refuse to attend training.
- refuse to follow leadership.

The congregation must have a biblical understanding of the offices of the church. The pastor is the spiritual and administrative leader of the church. As spiritual leader, he/she is to teach and preach the gospel and provide leadership in developing the various ministries as God directs.

Case Studies

The case studies in this training provide a forum that maximizes group discussion and interaction. This is a powerful way to help group members deal with issues in their own lives that might otherwise be ignored. Every potential leader will face conflict at one point or another. The case study approach focuses priority on conflict management and other issues. The point is not necessarily to resolve the issue to everyone's satisfaction or even to reach unanimity on what happened or ought to happen, but to engage people in thinking through the issues and contemplating how they can apply what they learned in their lives.

Case studies give an understanding of how to deal with troublesome situations. There are three levels of study in each case.

Level 1: This level deals with understanding the critical incident and the background of the event. The critical incident is the main problem that created the situation. Studying the background information is helpful in understanding the critical incident.

Level 2: This level involves the integrative, theological reflection on exegetical process. This process involves analysis and evaluation. The exegetical process involves interpreting the prevailing issues of the case. After the exegetical process is completed, the hermeneutics process is applied. Hermeneutics requires theological reflection on the issues. This process provides suggestive solutions to the issues in the case from a theological prospective.

Level 3: This level focuses on synthesis or judging the research, evaluating the ministry action and deciding about future ministry. The synthesis involves reviewing the decision that was made concerning the issues in the case, evaluating the actions that were taken, and determining how similar issues will be handled in the future.

Be mindful that the cases are not intended to provide an opportunity just to exchange human wisdom, but to wrestle with biblical teaching and its application to dilemmas of real people.

The Work and Ministry of the Church

> *It was he who gave some to be apostles, some to be prophets, some to be evangelists, and some to be pastors and teachers, to prepare God's people for works of*

> *service, so that the body of Christ may be built up (Ephesians 4:11–12).*

When describing the work and ministry of the church, it is important to remind the participants of Christ's original purpose for the church and the tasks He assigned His disciples before returning to His Father. As we look at the church today, our purpose and assignment has not changed. However, our strategies must change to meet the needs and demands of an ever darkening society.

The local assembly is the place where saints can grow and develop in ministry. Unfortunately, there is a vacuum of lay leadership within our churches. There are unregenerate congregations who have no personal encounter with Christ. They cannot see that Christ is the Head of the church and the Holy Spirit is the Director of the church. The church is the place where sinners find hope in Christ and learn the faith so well from the pastor/teacher that when Christ comes again, they will be ready to embrace Him and be with Him forevermore. The phenomenon is that far more people join the church than have joined Jesus Christ. The task of the militant church is to prepare the members for their place in the triumphant church. This task is completed through the local church where

God has sent gifted pastors and teachers to equip the saints for the work of ministry (Ephesians 4:7–16).

The perpetuation of the gospel of Christ, formed in the doctrines of the Word, and lived in life by practice is the work of the ministry. The involvement in missions at home and abroad, through social and educable experiences shows that the church, in her local expression, is not fearful of rubbing up against culture. Jesus has imposed upon us a territory of the world, and in that world, we are able to be salt and light (Matthew 5:14–16).[54]

The task of the militant church is to prepare the members for their place in the triumphant church.

Deacon's Ministry Training

This lesson is to help other laymen understand the role of the deacon. Deacons are the pastor's helpers (Acts 6:6–7) and are accountable to the pastor. The deacon is set apart to serve the needs of the members of the church. In order to serve the membership more effectively, members are assigned to the deacons' care. It is expected that deacons will call, visit and get to know members who are assigned to them. The deacons are expected to visit members during periods of sickness, death, or other crisis and inform the pastor when additional actions are needed.

The Deacon and His Calling

The origin and work of the deacon is rooted in at least five theological presuppositions:

1. Christ's concern for all people or the total needs of man
2. The recognition of man's limitations and inadequacies to meet his needs alone
3. The imperfection of the visible organized church structure (including the strength and weakness of men) to do its work and meet all the needs of the members at all times
4. The eternal cry of the needy when neglected or discriminated against by those in authority or when certain basic human needs are not met
5. An organized plan to strengthen the church, to spread its responsibilities among more of the members, and to establish a division of labor that assigns specific tasks to certain individuals

A person is not made a deacon just for the honor. The deacon is set apart to serve. He is committed to serve God and his fellowman. The office of deacon is not one of authority, but one of service. The position was originally established to preserve the spiritual fellowship of his church.

The deacon's function is that of an assistant to the pastor. He is chosen by the church at the suggestion of the pastor to do a threefold task as the need occurs:

1. To serve the needs of the church members
2. To be ready, prepared, and available for the opportunities and responsibilities to serve Christ throughout the church
3. To serve as an assistant and subordinate to the pastor of the church, working in cooperation with and being held responsible to the pastor

The Deacon's Relationship to the Church

The deacon and pastor comprise a team that should be most intimately connected and thoroughly cooperative in the work of the Lord and the service of the church. The characteristics that are necesary of a man who is selected to serve as a deacon are:

1. He must be willing to be all that God wants him to be.

2. He must be willing to do all the church wants him to do.
3. He must have earned his right to be respected as a Christian.
4. He must never be satisfied with himself as he is.
5. He must know God and the members of the church firsthand.
6. He must be aware of what he can become as the result of spiritual growth through prayer, study, and the grace of God.

Pastors and deacons share similar qualifications. Man does not set the leader's qualifications. God gave divine insight to Paul as he set forth qualities of spiritual life that pastors and deacons are to possess. There is a grave danger when the church lowers the qualifications of either of these Christian leaders.

The Deacon: Partner With His Pastor

When one is named a deacon of the church, he becomes a partner in service with his pastor. All persons need the emotional support that comes from others. The pastor has a right to expect support from all of the people—deacons and members. All of the people should expect support from the deacons, the pastor, and others in the fellowship. Pastors and deacons must adopt the team concept, *"For we are God's fellow workers" (1 Corinthians 3:9).*

In Christ's church, there should be no empire builders; there are no solo performers. The forward motion of the church in accomplishing the purposes of Christ is slowed or stopped when the pastor and deacons are not a team.

The Differences in Pastor and Deacon Leadership Roles

First Timothy 3 speaks of the kind of person both leaders are to be. They are to be spiritual men on a spiritual mission. Each should be in the process of *becoming*.

The church calls the pastor to be a generalist leader. In his leadership role, the pastor serves as a player-coach-enabler. He develops people. As generalist leader, the pastor leads the church to determine its spiritual mission.

Deacons are exemplary leaders. They serve as models for fellow Christians to follow. As exemplary leaders, deacons often serve behind the scene, out of the spotlight or central focus of activities. Following are some guidelines for deacons:

1. **Understand the Pastor and His Work**

   Being a pastor is like many other tasks in life, and yet it is unlike anything else in the world. It is being loved and unloved, wanted and unwanted, understood and misunderstood. At times it is heaven; at other times it is hell. The pastor needs friends. He needs someone who will keep his confidences and share with him during moments of loneliness. Deacons and other laity must understand the pastor and his work.

2. **Pray for the Pastor**

   Laity must lift up your pastor in daily prayers and breathe a silent prayer of thanksgiving for him and his ministry and mention his name in your private and public prayers. Laity must stop by the pastor's office and join him in prayer.

3. **Affirm the Pastor**

   Laity will be affirmed as they affirm and support the pastor. When deacons take the leadership in sponsoring the Pastor's Appreciation day, they are saying, "Pastor, we love you."

4. **Support the Pastor**

   Because the deacon is the pastor's moral and spiritual helper in service to the people, he should be supportive of his pastor. Encourage him. Defend him when he is criticized unfairly. Be frank with him when it is thought that he is mistaken, but support him.

5. **Enjoy Fellowship with the Pastor**

   The partnership or team concept means that laity and clergy can depend on each other. They must practice being open, honest, and loving in all relationships. The deacons are expected to be men of integrity, consecration, and wisdom. They should be knowledgeable of their duties and in full sympathy with the policies of their leaders.

The Deacon Ministry

The deacon seeks not his own will, but to know and do the will of the church, which he serves under Christ. The deacons help the pastor by being his/her moral and spiritual helpers in service to the people. The deacons help the church by:

1. Attending the services and participating in the work of the church
2. Supporting the financial program of the church
3. Encouraging the indifferent members and praising the faithful ones

4. Discouraging envy, backbiting, and strife
5. Refraining from gossip, and insisting that the truth be told about all matters
6. Guarding any confidences

The Deacon Translating His Qualifications into Service

God, in His divine wisdom, set the qualifications for a deacon high because the work of the deacon is spiritual in its nature. His service must be rendered from a heart of righteousness. Therefore, as a deacon serves, his actions consistently demonstrate that he is:

- **A Man of Honest Report** (Acts 6:13). He has a good reputation among those in the church as well as those outside the church.
- **Full of the Holy Spirit** (Acts 6:3). A deacon shows bigness of character in his spiritual outlook and personal dedication.
- **Full of Wisdom** (Acts 6:5). He has an ability to discern right or wrong and to stand for his convictions.
- **Full of Faith** (Acts 6:5). Like Stephen, a deacon's faith requires him to risk himself and his possessions for the Lord's sake.

- **Grave** (1 Timothy 3:8). He possesses Christian purpose and has great reverence for spiritual matters. As a result, his word carries weight.
- **Not Double-Tongued** (1 Timothy 3:8). A deacon is temperate in living, a steward of good influence, and does all to the glory of God.
- **Not Given Much to Wine** (1 Timothy 3:8). He is dependable and honest in relating to all persons publicly and privately.
- **Not Greedy of Filthy Lucre** (1 Timothy 3:9). He has the right attitude toward material possessions, never exploiting others for his own gain.
- **A Holder of the Faith** (1 Timothy 3:9). He gives strength to the church fellowship and possesses spiritual integrity beyond reproach.
- **Tested and Proven** (1 Timothy 3:10). He demonstrates his commitment to the ministry before being elected to serve as a deacon.
- **Blameless** (1 Timothy 3:10). No charge of wrong-doing can be successfully brought against him.
- **Head of a Christian Home** (1 Timothy 3:11–12). His family is well cared for, and his family relationships are healthy and growing.

- **The Husband of One Wife** (1 Timothy 3:12). He is faithfully devoted to one spouse and committed to the sanctity of marriage.
- **Ruler of His Children and His Household** (1 Timothy 3:12). He is loved and respected by all family members because he cares for them as Jesus cared for others.
- **Bold in Faith** (1 Timothy 3:13). He holds firmly to what he believes, taking every opportunity for ministry.[55]

The Vision of Leadership

The pastor is to tie together all that the participants have learned into a clear description of his vision of leadership for the church. The lay leaders' understanding and ownership of the vision is critical to equipping them to lead. I want the leaders around me to know my vision because the church does not accomplish its goals without this focus. Having and sharing a vision does more than drive a ministry, it also gives people vision and direction for their individual lives.

Leaders are expected to support the vision-established strategies for their given ministries and to carry out the mission of the church. Teamwork among leaders, ministries, and members is essential to accomplishing the vision. Ultimately, the vision of leadership of the Macedonia Baptist Church is to equip the laity for Christian leadership and empower armor bearers to serve in the next millennium. This is done through activating the resources God already has given the church. The vision for your church may be similar. If the vision is to come to fruition, then it must be communicated in such a way that the lay leaders can clearly and succinctly communicate it to others.

> *Write down the revelation and make it plain on tablets so that a herald may run with it (Habakkuk 2:2).*

Recognition and Awards

Particpants who successfully complete the Laity Leadership Training course should be recognized. I suggest having a graduation ceremony. It is good to announce the event several weeks in advance to allow family, friends, and guests to attend.

The program should begin with the graduates marching in and being seated together. The pastor should select one class member who exemplified outstanding achievement in attendance, completion of assignments, and class discussion to challenge the graduates during the ceremony. Immediately after the challenge, the pastor and a designee present each graduate with a certificate of achievement (preferably a plaque). As each name is called, the graduates march in front of the church congregation to receive their plaques and a congratulatory handshake from the pastor.

The Benefit of Equipping

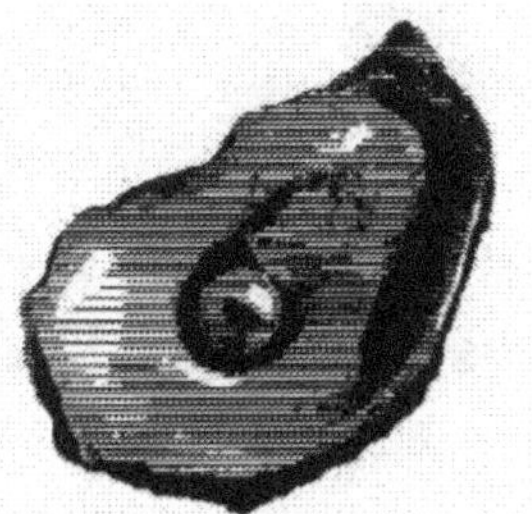

The results of a study showed that the Laity Leaderhip Training program at Macedonia Baptist Church had a significant and positive impact on the church's ministry. It created enthusiasm and motivation among the participants. Ninety-eight percent of the surveys were returned. Sixty-seven percent rated the quality of material presented in class excellent, and 29 percent rated the materials good. According to the survey responses, 74 percent rated the program excellent in terms of fulfilling their expectations, and 22 percent rated the course good. Based upon the survey results, the overall training program was effective and beneficial to the Macedonia Baptist Church.

Based on research, survey forms, interviews, and overall program evaluation, I have drawn the following conclusions about the Laity Leadership

Training program and the effect it had on present and potential leaders at Macedonia Baptist Church:

1. **The program provided a forum for introducing new ideas and change to the church's leadership.**

I have pastored Macedonia Baptist Church for twelve years. There have been many changes since I began serving as pastor. The Laity Leadership Training provides a platform to teach the vision to the church's leaders. More than 98 percent of the participants have embraced the church's vision as demonstrated by their financial support, eagerness to assume leadership roles, and general support of the vision. This training enabled me to teach new ideas as well as test the climate for the level of support for meaningful change.

The program setting provided a forum for dialogue about new ideas and the impact upon the congregation. The figures in the survey show a positive way to open the line of communication for change among potential leaders. When asked, "Did the instructor utilize the valuable input of the students in the class?" Sixty-four percent of the participants responded excellent, while 32 percent responded good, 2 percent average, and 2 percent gave no response.

2. The program helped believers identify their gifts.

The New Testament teaches that spiritual gifts are endowed by the Holy Spirit and given to every believer for the purpose of building up the church and its ministry. The training used lessons regarding the paradigms of "Being, Becoming, and Doing" to focus on individual spiritual gifts.

> *It was he who gave some to be apostles, some to be prophets, some to be evangelists, and some to be pastors and teachers, to prepare God's people for works of service, so that the body of Christ may be built up (Ephesians 4:11–12).*

The training gave participants the opportunity to focus on their own individual gifts. Of the forty-one participants, thirty-five responded positively to the gift of leadership. Ninety-one percent stated the course allowed them to examine themselves more closely. Although the course was a leadership training course, participants seem to have been challenged to discover and employ their various gifts.

3. The program created a pool of qualified leaders in the church.

Of the forty-one participants in the training program, twenty-one were already serving in leadership positions, while nineteen were potential leaders. These created a pool for future leadership.

Because leaders at Macedonia Baptist Church serve a two-year tenure, there is a constant need for a pool of leaders who are ready to assume the role of leadership. This training has produced a ready resource of servant-leaders who are prepared to take their place in the local church.

4. The program equipped believers for everyday living.

Many of the participants did not know what to expect at the beginning of the training. After the training program, their responses indicated that a majority had not only received training for leadership in the church, but also for everyday living. Some realized that the gifts of the Spirit were not only for use within the church. Some who possessed the gift of teaching were motivated to use their gift in their homes. Some who possessed the gift of helping learned that it was important for them to use their gifts in the office, workplace, and various walks of life. One participant wrote, "This course has made me more aware of my actions in all things that I do." Another stated, "This course has not only helped me in church, but also on the job." Of the total participants, 91 percent responded excellent to the question: How well has this course allowed you to examine yourself more closely as a leader/Christian? Seven percent responded well, while 2 percent responded average, which indicated overwhelming consensus on the impact this training had in the everyday life of the participants.

5. The program equipped believers for the work of evangelism and ministry.

The study revealed that many of the participants were encouraged to bring others to Christ. Comments were made regarding increased confidence in sharing God's Word with others. Evidently, there are more Laity Leadership graduates now participating in the church's evangelistic campaigns.

6. The program prepared others to teach.

The Macedonia Baptist Church believes that teaching is an essential ministry for preparing believers for successful living and evangelism. We believe that teaching is the "heart" of the mission of the church. Those who teach must first be taught. There was a great need for skilled, effective teachers to support the ministry of the church. The Laity Leadership Training also created a pool for teachers. Fifteen of the forty-one participants are now engaged in the teaching ministry of the church. Just as Jesus trained His disciples; as Paul trained Silas, Barnabas, and Timothy; and as Moses trained Joshua, so must the pastor train the laity. By doing so, the church will reap great benefits in its efforts to further the ministry of Christ.

7. The program strengthened and unified the church toward a common vision.

I have witnessed cohesiveness toward our vision. I discovered through the training that when the pastor knows the people and shares the vision, it helps them know the pastor and understand where he is leading. This training gave the participants the desire to follow directions and learn from their leader. Many of the participants stated that prior to the training, they did not understand the mission of the church. Some had not fully embraced the mission statement and the vision of the pastor.

The following statements represent a selective sampling of participants' responses regarding how the training program helped to clarify their roles and responsibilities within the church's vision:

> *This course has allowed laity the chance to know what is expected of us and how we affect each organization. The course has given us direct duties and responsibilities for each ministry so that we may know our goals and what we are supposed to be doing for the church.*

> *This course has made me more helpful to the pastor, the vision, and the church.*

> *The church's mission statement speaks of commitment to spreading the gospel (saving souls) and this class has allowed me to get in touch with me in order to help others.*

There are other positive statements from the survey. As pastor, I have witnessed how greatly the church has benefited from this training. Since the leadership training, there has been an increase in membership and finances over the past two years. Laypersons tend to give more to the church and the ministry when they are committed. Those who completed the training better understand the mission.

The open-ended questions on the survey revealed a spirit of motivation and understanding of the vision of the church. There were only two "no" responses out of the forty-one participants to the question: Has this course furthered our aim as a church to achieve the mission statement? Some wrote about understanding their own responsibility to the church; others wrote about the clarity of the mission statement. The responses reported an overall positive impact regarding the unity of the church. Some said they were being a greater help to the pastor.

Below are some comments from participants, which suggest that positive growth has taken place in the church:

> *This course has helped our church to be on one accord with our mission.*

> *The information was concise and clear. Definitions on the role of different organizational leaders in the church show that we help and work together as members of God's family. Unity was presented as important to the church and to achieve our missions and goals."*

This course has increased our awareness to stay on track. I also believe that those of us who participated in this course will share what we have learned and experienced with others; it will motivate our fellow members.

I believe it has encouraged us to pull together as a team to reach Commitment 2000 goals and other goals of the church.

This course has helped me to be more committed to the work of the church, helping to fulfill the goals of the mission statement.

The pastor's vision, the acceptance of the Lord, the church's mission statement and working together should keep Macedonia growing and each individual as well.

This course, I feel, has drawn us all together in our unified effort to achieve the goal that has been sent down from God to our pastor.

There were other positive comments concerning the impact of the training on unifying the church as a body. The training has unified the church spiritually.

Our trained leaders understand that Jesus Christ is the center of life, church ministry, and leadership. When leaders are spiritually-centered, they understand spiritually-centered leadership. This type of leadership blesses the congregation.

The participants were asked the question: How well did the course help you grow spiritually? There were only two "none" responses and 89 percent responded "excellent," while 9 percent responded "good" on the survey. The comments regarding the question were positive. Some talked about how the course gave them a new view of their own spirituality. Some spoke seriously about how they must keep focused on being. The improved spiritual climate the training created within the church is evidenced by increased attendance and a warm, genuine fellowship.

8. The program equipped believers inside and outside of the church.

Survey results indicated that the program has made a considerable positive impact on participants not only in church, but also outside of the church. Leadership is not a one-time effort; rather, leadership must be personified constantly. Participants indicated that the program gave them confidence on their jobs and in their personal lives. One layperson in particular stated that the course helped him to become more honest, trustworthy, and loyal, and gave him a desire to live so others can see Christ in his life.

9. The program distributed the workload among many members.

The purpose of this training is to involve laypersons in the work of the ministry. The training at Macedonia Baptist Church has successfully engaged leaders in the work of ministry. There were nineteen potential leaders at the time of training. All but four are now engaged in some area of leadership within the church. Pastors must learn that a few people do not have to carry the bulk of the load. By training a variety of leaders, the work of ministry becomes more effectively spread among many members.

10. The program increased support for the church's ministry and pastor.

During the twelve weeks of training, I was able to teach the participants about the church's ministry and the pastor's need to have a support base among the leadership. The participant's responses to the open-ended questions on the survey overwhelmingly revealed that for a majority, the impact of this training increased their support of the church, its ministry, and the pastor.

The desired outcomes (program goals) served as a guide for the study. Some of the results were beyond anticipation. The degree of success realized within each domain varied considerably. The participants were asked, "What did you find most valuable in the course?" Forty of the 41 participants replied, "Spiritual growth." Fifteen of the participants made positive comments about the teaching of the paradigm of "Being, Becoming, and Doing." Following are some of their comments:

> *The paradigm on "Being, Becoming and Doing" was the most valuable tool used in this course. It helped me to realize where I am in Christ. Through some of the most difficult times, I questioned myself and understood why I was going through things. I realize it was necessary in order to grow spiritually and to become what God desires me to be.*

> *The paradigm on "Being" really challenged me.*

The explanation on the paradigm on "Being," descriptions of various church ministries, and clear definitions of theological terminology were most valuable in the course.

The information presented concerning a person's growth centering around "Being" before you attempt to "Do" was very valuable. The in-depth presentations concerning the qualities of a good leader vs. an individual leader were interesting. The Scriptures given were very helpful in understanding the material presented in class.

I valued learning about the development phase of Christian leadership, "Being, Becoming, and Doing." I also enjoyed learning about church administration, such as the role of the pastor, deacons, ministers and laity; and learning how to apply the case study principles in providing leadership as well in my daily Christian life.

I valued the paradigm on "Being" and knowing who I am first.

> *The paradigm of "Being, Becoming and Doing" was enjoyable. I hadn't thought of it in the way it was taught in this class.*

> *I really enjoyed the importance of "Being" before "Becoming." This really causes me to do some soul searching.*

> *The role of a leader and his/her attitude were valuable to me. I also valued the paradigm of "Being, Becoming, and Doing."*

> *I valued the understanding of accepting who you are, and "Being" as it related to growing as a Christian.*

These comments conclusively show that the training course had a spiritual impact on the participants.

The case studies were valuable tools in the training course. The survey results indicate that 86 percent rated the benefits of the case study approach as excellent, while 14 percent responded good. Some of their comments about the value of the case studies were:

> *The case studies were valuable. It allowed me to look at different situations that may happen in my ministry and in my day-to-day life. But it showed me how to handle it.*

> *I really enjoyed the case studies; I found working on the case studies to be very valuable. The studies helped me to understand why people do some of the things they do rather than always looking at who's right or wrong.*

Finally, the participants were asked what things were of least value in the course. The responses to this question provided much insight regarding the effectiveness of the course, and served as a guide for future adjustments. The comments from the majority of the participants were positive. The responses ranged from "Everything was valuable" to specific observations. Some stated that going over the ministries in the church was invaluable. Following are some of their comments:

> *All things in the course were valuable because all the information applied to my life as a Christian. It assisted me in evaluating our relationship and obligations to Christ. It helped me to be aware of my responsibility as a leader and as a Christian.*

> *Everything that was taught was very important to being in a leadership position.*

Everything in the course was valuable to me. There was not a night that I wasn't inspired and encouraged in the ministry.

I feel that all the information was valuable to my spiritual growth as a leader in the church and community around me.

There were comments that stated the course was too long. Others felt that the scheduling sometimes conflicted with other activities going on at the church. When asked to make any other comment or specific suggestions to improve the course and/or teaching method, only twenty-nine participants responded. Each statement provided valuable information that would improve the training program in the future. Some of the suggestions were to:

- Videotape the sessions for home study or for students to use as a resource tool.
- Assign outside reading and research for students to present articles to the class on church leadership for discussion.
- Use visual aids.
- Have everyone write a case study and lead the class discussion with the instructor looking on.

Although there were some concerns about the course, the overall sentiment was that Laity Leadership

Training is needed in every church. The comments listed below reflect the positive impact this course had on our participants and the effect it can have on any church.

> *This course has truly been a blessing to me. I can truly say that I grew spiritually over these past weeks.*

> *Rev. Walker's lessons were well prepared. It seems that he anticipated questions and had many real life examples to include as clarification points.*

> *All elements of the course were simply good.*

> *I know everything or person can stand improvement, but this course is a class "A." You can't find any better teaching method than this.*

> *I valued learning about the development phase of Christian leadership, "Being, Becoming, and Doing." I also enjoyed learning about church administration (i.e., the role of the pastor, deacons, ministers and laity) and learning how to apply the case study principles in*

providing leadership as well as in my daily Christian life.

I valued getting a clearer understanding of the Pastor's vision and expectations of leaders within the church. The training manual was great, and helped me to get a better understanding of the church directory.

I valued the fellowship and the breakdown of the church directory. Learning the roles of some of the ministries and leaders, learning how I can be of help to my pastor, and learning what God and my pastor expect of me as a leader really broadened my horizons.

The characteristics and expectations of leadership were valuable to me.

All things in the course were valuable because all the information applied to my life as a Christian. It assisted me in evaluating our relationships and obligations to Christ. It helped me to be aware of my responsibility as a leader and as a Christian. We are responsible for the lost and fallen brothers and sisters in Christ.

I have made a stronger commitment to my ministry. Sometimes what others expect from this ministry can make you question what the ministry is about. But when it comes straight from the pastor, it makes the vision real.

I'm looking to make my involvement directly impact our mission statement in a spiritually positive way.

It made me take a look at how serious leadership is and to look at myself spiritually.

The course showed me how to interact with others within this ministry. It has given me the ability to work with others within my chosen ministry.

The results of this Laity Leadership Training are clearly stated in the comments received from the participants. Equipping the laity for christian leadership will impact individual lives as well as the church.

For you are a people holy to the LORD your God. The LORD your God has chosen you out of all the peoples on the face of the earth to be his people, his treasured possession (Deuteronomy 7:6).

The Laity in the New Millennium

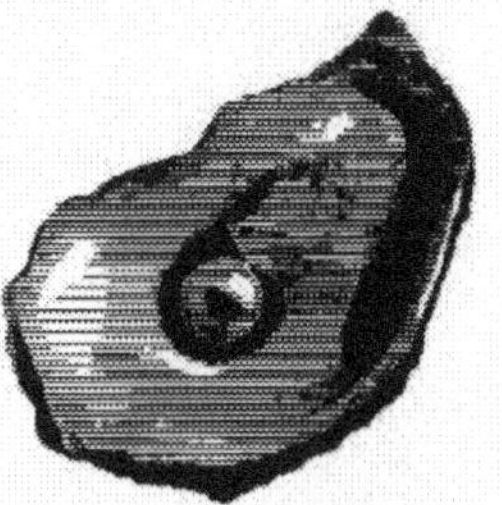

We must train the laity in our churches, give them important things to do, and let them do them. The church becomes stronger when the pastor does not have to see to it that everything is done, or does not have to do it himself. Hans Ruedi Weber in his book, *The Rediscovering of the Laity*, places the laity in the proper perspective.

> The growing interest I have in the laity is not to be interpreted as an attempt to transform the laity into something larger than it is, or to seek recognition in the church. Rather, my interest is a means to supplement an overburdened and understaffed ordained ministry.

The laity is really the *laos*, which means the people of God in the entire world, including, of course, those who have been ordained.[56] The laity shares in Christ's ministry to the world. This was also the concern of Oldhams, which was widely publicized in a statement adopted by the Central Committee of the World Council of Churches in 1956, on the ministry of the laity in the world. In reaction to the traditionally prevailing concept of the church with its focus on organization, activities, and buildings, the emphasis is now sometimes too exclusively laid on the presence of the laity in the structures and institutions of secular society. In rediscovering the laity in this new millennium, often the role of the laity is gauged by finance and attendance only. However, there remains a lot of work to do in the area of equipping God's people for ministry. The basic intention is to gather God's people in the assembly in order to strengthen them and send them out for witness and service.[57] God gives His gifts in variety to His people. One of the primary callings of the church is to discover and develop these gifts for the world.

The laity in the new millennium face the challenge of breaking traditions and meeting the needs of multiple generations. Fortunately, there are many excellent leadership development resources available to assist in equipping lay leaders. Don and Katie Fortune share helpful tips for equipping the laity in their book, *Discover Your God-Given Gifts*. The authors provide extensive and insightful self-help forms that will help laity recognize their gift.[58]

Ford's *Transforming Leadership*, Wilkes' *Jesus on Leadership*, and Greenleaf's *Servant-Leadership*, provide a model for equipping saints with the right attitude. These three sources are crucial to the kind of leadership which Jesus modeled.

Transforming Leadership provides a good introduction to contemporary Christians about leadership and a creative response open for new possibilities. Ford addresses the rapid change in a complex society. He realizes that there is a need for bold leadership, which serves as a launching pad to establish a laity group. Ford recognizes leaders as servants, which was Jesus' model for leadership. Ford acknowledges Gardner's essay, which describes leadership and power as the capacity to ensure the outcome one wishes and to prevent those that one does not wish to happen. Ford further writes that Jesus turned the power side upside down, measuring greatness by the ability to serve.[59]

Wilkes' contemporary work, *Jesus on Leadership*, modeled the style of leadership that I feel is crucial for laity within the local church. Wilkes discusses seven principles of servant leadership which I feel are part of the leadership problem within the local church. Many churches struggle because they lack servant leaders. Head tables have replaced the towel and washbasin as symbols of leadership among God's people.[60]

The best evidence of successful servant leadership is demonstrated when those who are served grow as people.

Greenleaf further confronts the problems of servant leaders functioning in various fields. According to Greenleaf, the servant-leader is servant-first. The difference manifests itself in the care taken by the servant-leader to make sure that other high priority needs are being served. The best evidence of successful servant leadership is demonstrated when those who are served grow as people. While being served, they become healthier, wiser, freer, more autonomous, and more likely to become servants themselves.[61]

Greenleaf urges followers to refuse to follow any leader who is not a servant leader.[62] The well-known authors of *The Leadership Challenge*, Kouzes and Posner, wrote in

Credibility: How Leaders Gain and Lose It, Why People Demand It:

> Leaders we admire do not place themselves at the center; they place others there. They do not seek the attention of people; they give it to others. They do not focus on satisfying their own aims and desires; they look for ways to respond to the needs and interests of their constituents. They are not self-centered; they concentrate on the constituent.
>
> Leaders serve a purpose and the people who have made it possible for them to lead in serving a purpose. Leaders strengthen credibility by demonstrating that they are not in it for themselves; instead, they have the interests of the institution, department, or team and its constituents at heart. Being a servant may not be what many leaders had in mind when they choose to take responsibility for the vision and direction of their church, but serving others is the most glorious and rewarding of all leadership tasks.[63]

Bethel, a motivational speaker, says:

> In order to make a difference, we must be willing to serve. Real service has a

> high value. We can have real impact on people and problems if we contribute our time, emotions, energy, and effort. When we contribute to the well-being of others, our joy and fulfillment are immeasurable. The philosophy of history's leaders who have had a positive effect on our world has been one of service.[64]

Invariably, servant-leaders have advanced mankind. Only when service for a common good is the primary purpose, are you truly leading.[65] In Christian circles, this style of leadership has been further described and developed by Greenslade, Miller, Hildebrand and most extensively in Habecker's, *Leading With a Follower's Heart*.

A study at Fuller Theological Seminary led by Clinton shows that few leaders finish well. Because of the speed of change today with urbanization, globalization, computerization, feminization, values, confusion, and many other factors, we have to look at new ways to view and develop leadership. The church's bottom-line imperative is to unlock the laity so that it can achieve at its fullest capacity. The rise of seven-day-a-week churches indicates that the role of leadership is, in fact, spreading throughout the church, rather than being focused on one individual pastor. Jesus said:

> *The greatest among you will be your servant. For whoever exalts himself will be humbled, and whoever humbles himself will be exalted (Matthew 23:11–12).*

One other finding in Clinton's study was that significant relationships were very important to finishing well. Older styles of leadership often did not allow for nurturing, mentors, personal bonds of directors, and systems of support that provide health and wholeness for individuals and institutions.[66]

The church's bottom-line imperative is to unlock the laity so that it can achieve at its fullest capacity.

Maxwell, a well-known author who is extremely gifted in the area of leadership, provided a map in his book, *Developing the Leader Within You*. He showed how to develop the vision, value, influence, and motivation required for successful leadership.[67] This book is crucial in helping laity develop the leader within them. He has also written a helpful book entitled *Developing the Leaders Around You,* in which he discusses the mentoring aspects of ministry and what equipping the laity is all about. This work teaches the laity practical principles for helping the pastor by sharing leadership responsibility.[68]

Miller, in *The Empowered Leader,* suggested that to empower people, they must feel significant. They must be taught that learning and competence matter because they inspire community and incite vision.[69]

The apostle Paul laid the foundation for layman in the New Testament. He practiced servant-leader approach to leadership development and church planting. His life and ministry demonstrated the incarnation of servant-leadership in the way he selected and trained leaders, and established churches. Paul saw himself as a servant of Christ and a steward. He encouraged people to serve Christ and others, and he encouraged leadership development according to a person's giftedness, rather than one's position.

> *It was he who gave some to be apostles, some to be prophets, some to be evangelists, and some to be pastors and teachers, to prepare God's people for works of service, so that the body of Christ may be built up until we all reach unity in the faith and in the*

knowledge of the Son of God and become mature, attaining to the whole measure of the fullness of Christ (Ephesians 4:11–13).

The handwriting is on the wall. We must recognize that there is a new pearl in the pew. We are challenged to minister to several generations at one time in the church. In his book, *Transformational Leadership*, Phillip Lewis talks about the pre-boomers, baby boomers, and baby busters. Each generation has their own peculiarities.[70] We must be able to transform ministry to meet the needs of the congregation. The pre-boomers must understand that they put the church in a state of barrenness when they refuse to change and grow. They believe their heritage has made them complete; therefore, they do not see the need for a church to change leadership, ministries, or to be led by the Spirit of God. They are barren, not by nature, but by choice. I have seen members fight the leader and use all within their being to hinder anything that is new and violates their *sacred cows*. It is a disgrace when so-called senior saints quit praying, start playing, and end up straying.

The church must recognize that there is a new pearl in the pew. There is a different person in the pew now than there was twenty or thirty years ago.

The seasons of one's spiritual pilgrimage allow places and times of barrenness, but also times of birth and new revelation. We need to tap on the window of methodology, establish priorities for our time, and redefine what success in ministry looks like. We are called to go to a place we do not know to break with traditions instead of clinging to comfortable and familiar methods in order that the message might live to seek the will of Christ.

It is time the church recognizes that she has been called to effectiveness, not activity; to fruitfulness, not faithfulness; to relevancy, not ritual; to truth, not traditions.

If we do what we have always done, we will get what we have always gotten. Developing the pearls in the pew is not without pain and carries a price of commitment. The church can no longer suffer by allowing persons to hold positions with wrong motives, and hidden agendas. The church can no longer suffer by allowing dead, traditional-minded people to set the tone and status quo for ministry. It is time the church recognizes that she has been called to effectiveness, not activity; to fruitfulness, not faithfulness; to relevancy, not ritual; to truth, not traditions.

God is raising a leadership who is set apart for the gospel of Christ (Romans 1:1). Like Paul we can say:

> *I have become its servant by the commission God gave me to present to you the word of God in its fullness – the mystery that has been kept hidden for ages and generations, but is now disclosed to the saints. To them God has chosen to make known among the Gentiles the glorious riches of this mystery, which is Christ in you, the hope of glory. We proclaim him, admonishing and teaching everyone with all wisdom, so that we may present everyone perfect in Christ (Colossians 1:25–28).*

I am aware that many in our churches are pretending to be something they are not. They are like puppets on a string that have no will of their own, but fit easily in the category of man-pleaser. In I Corinthians 16:13, God says, *"Stand firm in the faith."* In Galatians 5:1, He says, *"Stand firm, then, and do not let yourselves be burdened again by a yoke of slavery."* In Philippians 1:27, He says, *"Stand firm in one spirit."* In I Thessalonians 3:8, He says, *"For now we really live, since you are standing firm in the Lord."*

These verses do not suggest a weak, spineless Christian who is afraid to look the devil in his eye and boldly rebuke him.

We must step to the next level and recognize that God is restoring the ministry of the apostle and prophet to His church.

This is a season of boldness. We must boldly walk in the authority God has given us. To stand fast in the faith means to be bold for the Lord, regardless of what anyone says or thinks. Horace Bushnell stated, "There are two great virtues in life—to bear and to dare." Every believer of Christ would do well to incorporate these words, bear and dare, into his daily living. We need to bear a consistent testimony for Christ and dare to walk in our destiny. We must be determined to walk in our God-given assignment daily. We must step to the next level and recognize that God is restoring the ministry of the apostle and prophet to His church. The true apostle and prophet are not solitary. God has called them to work in unity together. They are the foundation upon which God builds the body of

Christ. They are fathers in the Lord who seek not their own glory, but the glory of Christ. There is a deep longing for covering and fathering for the sake of connection, networking, and accountability. We are seeing fellowships forming everywhere with a resurgence of apostolic ministry.

The priesthood of believers is being rediscovered as Christians accept their call into various areas of ministry. There are bishops almost everywhere, which suggests that saints are conforming to the New Testament order and spiritual authority. There is a yearning for covering under a ministry. Pastors desire to be covered by a bishop with an apostolic anointing. Laity desire to be covered by a pastor or bishop that believes in the apostolic move of God, and a leader who will lay hands on the sick, speak in tongues, and speak destiny and purpose into their lives.

> *Then we will no longer be infants, tossed back and forth by the waves, and blown here and there by every wind of teaching and by the cunning and craftiness of men in their deceitful scheming. Instead, speaking the truth in love, we will in all things grow up into him who is the Head, that is, Christ (Ephesians 4:14–15).*

We must be determined to stand fast in this season of shaking, shifting, and sifting *"until we all reach unity in the faith and in the knowledge of the Son of God and become mature, attaining to the whole measure of the fullness of Christ" (Ephesians 4:13).*

A true story comes out of history. In the days when the ruling passion of the Roman emperor, Nero, was the extermination of Christians, there lived a stalwart band of soldiers known as the emperor's wrestlers. In the great amphitheater, they upheld the arms of the emperors against all challengers. Before each contest, they stood before the emperor's throne. Then, through the courts of Rome rang the cry, "We the wrestlers, wrestling for thee O' emperor, to win for thee the victory and from thee the victor's crown." When the great Roman army was sent to fight in far away Gaul, no soldiers were braver or more loyal than this band of wrestlers, led by their centurion Vespasian. But news reached Nero that many of these men had accepted the Christian faith. To be a Christian meant death, even to those who served Nero. Therefore, this decree was dispatched to Vespasian, if there be any among the soldiers who cling to the faith of the Christians, they must die. It was with sinking heart that Vespasian the centurion read the emperor's message.

Yet, he knew he had to perform his duty. He called the soldiers to gather and asked the question, "Are there any among you who cling to the faith of the Christians? If so, let him step forward." Forty wrestlers instantly stepped forward two paces, respectfully saluted, and stood at attention.[71]

Vespasian was surprised. He had not expected this. He read the decree from the emperor and pled with the men to renounce this false faith. Not one of the forty moved. "Alright," said Vespasian, "I command that you march out upon the Lake of Ice, and I shall leave you there to the mercy of the elements. Fires will be waiting to welcome any who are willing to renounce this false faith."

The forty wrestlers were stripped, and then without a word they wheeled and falling into columns of four marched toward the Lake of Ice. As they marched, they broke into chorus with the old chant of the arena, "Forty wrestlers wrestling for thee, O' Christ to win for thee the victory and from thee the victor's crown." All through the long hours of the night Vespasian waited by the campfire for the men to return. As morning drew near, one figure overcome by exposure crept quietly toward the fire. In the extremity of his suffering, he had renounced his Lord.

Still faintly, but clearly out of the darkness came the song, "Thirty-nine wrestlers wrestling for thee, O' Christ to win for thee the victory and from thee the victor's crown."

Vespasian looked at the figure drawing close to the fire, and then he looked out into the darkness from whence the song of faith came. Once again he looked and it is very possible that he saw a greater light shining in the darkness. Off came the helmet, down went his shield, and he sprang upon the ice crying, "Forty wrestlers wrestling for thee, O' Christ to win for thee the victory and from thee the victor's crown." And again the number of God's forty singing wrestlers was complete.[72]

I want my faith to match this faithful body of men who were undaunted by the temptation to deny Jesus. I must constantly tell myself that I am a pearl. I will not be bogged down by the cares of this life, not knowing the power and liberty I have in the cross. You must not sell out to Satan. Sell out to Jesus, for in Him the rewards are not only real, but everlasting.

Appendices

Appendix A: Letter to Participants 140

Appendix B: Attendance Log 142

Appendix C: Laity Leadership Training Manual . .143

Appendix D: Course Evaluation 159

Appendix E: Graduate Certificate 161

Letter to Participants

Your Church's Name
Your Church's Address
Phone: 999-999-9999 • Fax: 999-444-4444

Date

Dear Brother or Sister _____________:

I greet you in the name of our Lord and Savior, Jesus Christ. With the vision on the horizon and the ministries growing everyday, God has revealed to me to first **empower His people**, and secondly, to **equip laity for leadership**.

> *It was he who gave some to be apostles, some to be prophets, some to be evangelists, and some to be pastors and teachers, to prepare God's people for works of service, so that the body of Christ may be built up until we all reach unity in the faith and in the knowledge of the Son of God and become mature, attaining to the whole measure of the fullness of Christ (Ephesians 4:11–13).*

God has given me **the vision**, and it has been written and spoken. My vision in this endeavor is to equip laity for Christian Leadership. These leaders must have a personal relationship with God, for God would not give a person the **work** if they did not know Him on a personal level. Therefore, I have personally chosen members who I have observed and feel that with proper training, tutelage and the anointing of God, can provide effective Christian leadership as we move forward into the vision of our church.

With this in mind, I am personally asking for your time, loyalty, labor, and dedication to enroll in our Laity Leadership Training course, instructed by your pastor. The course is designed for future leaders of the church, and will require a partnership between pastor and leaders. During this training, a "teacher/student" relationship will not exist, but rather one of colleagues working together to build the kingdom of Christ.

This course will begin on _______________________, and will continue every Thursday for 12 weeks. The completion and graduation date is tentatively scheduled for _________________. All classes will begin promptly at 6:30 p.m., and conclude at approximately 9:00 p.m. Attendance at all classes is essential. Course materials will be provided.

In conclusion, please pray first and seek God's direction. Remember, to whom much is given, much is required (Luke 12:48). Please advise my Administrative Assistant of your decision to enroll in this course no later than ___________________. May God bless you, and may heaven shine upon you.

Yours in Christ,

Pastor

Attendance Log

Laity Leadership Training Attendance Log

Place a check under the date by the name of each participant who is present.

Name	Date	Date	Date	Date	Date	Date	Date	Date

Laity Leadership Training Participant's Manual

by

Dr. John H. Walker, Pastor

Table of Contents

Course Orientation 146

Expectations

Objectives

Relevance

Course Introduction 148

What is Laity?

The Pastor's Theology of Ministry

The Prerequisite of Leadership (Being) 149

The Preparation of Leadership (Becoming) 150

The Practice of Leadership (Doing) 153

Deacon's Ministry Training 156

The Vision of Leadership 158

Course Orientation

Expectations

Attendance (How much?)

Participation (What kind?)

Supplies (What should I bring?)

Will there be tests, reports, case studies, etc.?

Objectives

The objectives of the Laity Leadership Training course are to:

- Prepare ministry leaders for the 21st century.
- Create a pool of trained leaders to carry out the vision of this church.

Relevance

Why was I selected?

What will this training provide my church, my pastor, and me?

Course Introduction

What is Laity?

The Pastor's Theology of Ministry

The Prerequisite of Leadership

"Being a Leader"

Salvation

Faith

Key Points

The Preparation of Leadership

"Becoming a Leader"

Training

A Leader's Daily Requirement

Leader's Helping to Carry the Load

1. Becoming a Sounding Board

2. Possessing a Leadership Mindset

3. Developing Others for Leadership

A Dream Team of Leaders

1. Qualities of a Dream Team

2. Leader of a Dream Team

3. Potential of a Dream Team

The Practice of Leadership

"Doing as a Leader"

The Four Principles of Christian Leadership

1. ____
2. ____
3. ____
4. ____

Case Study(ies)

We will look at the following three levels when analyzing a case study.

Level 1: Description of the Event

A. The Critical Incident or Event

B. Background of the Event

Level 2: Integrative Theological Reflection

A. Exegetical Process (Analysis and Evaluation)

B. Hermeneutical Process (Reach, Reflection, and Interpretation)

Level 3: Synthesis

A. Judging the Research

B. Evaluating the Ministry Action

C. Decisions About Future Ministry

Case Study(ies)

The Work and Ministry of Our Church

Deacon's Ministry Training

The Deacon and His Calling

The Deacon: Partner With His Pastor

The Differences in Pastor and Deacon Leadership Roles

The Deacon Ministry

The Deacon Translating His Qualifications Into Service

The Vision of Leadership

Key Points

Laity Leadership Training Course Evaluation

This evaluation is confidential. Do not sign your name.

Age:	**Sex:**	**How long have you been a member of this church?**
Position: __Officer __Leader __Layman		
Occupation:		
Education: __High School __College (2 yr.) __College (4 yr.) __Masters __Doctorate		

Rate each item by circling your response.

Excellent (E) Good (G) Average (A) Poor (P) Undecided (U)

ITEM	E	G	A	P	U
1. Course introduction	4	3	2	1	0
2. Clarity of course objectives	4	3	2	1	0
3. Instructor's knowlege of subject	4	3	2	1	0
4. Quality of materials	4	3	2	1	0
5. Instructor's poise and demeanor	4	3	2	1	0
6. Use of time	4	3	2	1	0
7. Usefulness of visual aids	4	3	2	1	0
8. Usefulness of case study(ies)	4	3	2	1	0
9. Benefit of writing a case study	4	3	2	1	0
10. Stimulus to closely examine yourself as a Christian leader	4	3	2	1	0

ITEM	E	G	A	P	U
11. The instructor's use of students' input	4	3	2	1	0
12. Explanation of theological terminology	4	3	2	1	0
13. The instructor being prepared for each session	4	3	2	1	0
14. Your spiritual growth	4	3	2	1	0
15. The course fulfilling your expectations	4	3	2	1	0

16. What part(s) of the training was most valuable?

17. What part(s) of the training was least valuable?

18. How has this course affected you in your role in the ministry?

19. How has this course furthered our church's effort to achieve our mission statement?

20. What other comments or specific suggestions do you have to improve the course and/or teaching methods?

Your Church's Name

Pastor ____________ certifies the completion of all curriculum requirements and therefore confers upon

____

the honor of

Laity Leadership Graduate

Christian Leadership Course

Presented on the ___ day of _________ two thousand ___

____

Pastor's Name

Notes

Introduction

1. Geoffrey Guns, *Spiritual Leadership*, (Lithonia: Orman Press, 2000), 67.

2. Ibid., 68.

3. J. Oswald Sanders, *Spiritual Leadership*, (Chicago: Moody Press, 1967), 15–16.

4. Ibid., 17.

5. E. L. Thomas, *Guide to Successful Leadership*, (Milwaukee: Calvary Witnessing Voice), 16.

6. Thomas, *Guide to Successful Leadership*, 17.

7. Ibid.

8. Ibid.

9. Ibid.

Making of a Pearl

10. Perry, *Getting the Church on Target*, 105.

11. Ibid., 106.

12. Stephen Charles Neill and Hans-Ruedi Weber, *The Layman in Christian History*, (Philadelphia: Westminster Press, 1963), 15.

13. Ibid.

14. George Hunston Williams, *The Ancient Church,* (Philadelphia: Westminster, 1963), 28.

15. Ibid., 30.

16. Ibid., 31.

17. Ibid.

18. Ibid., 32.

19. Ibid., 31.

20. Ibid., 32.

21. Ibid.

22. William H. C. Frend, *The Church of the Roman Empire,* (Philadelphia: Westminster, 1963), 66.

23. Ibid.

24. Ibid., 81.

25. Ibid., 82.

26. Christopher N. L. Brook, *The Church of the Middle Ages,* (Philadelphia: Westminster, 1963), 111.

27. Ibid.

28. C. R. Cheney, *From Becket to Langton*, (Manchester, 1956), 155–156 where the texts from Deuteronomy and Galatians are also cited.

29. Brook, *The Church of the Middle Ages,* 132.

30. E. Gordon Rupp, *The Age of The Reformation,* (Philadelphia: Westminster, 1963), 139.

31. Ibid.

32. Ibid., 143.

33. Martin Schmidt, *The Continent of Europe,* (Philadelphia: Westminster, 1963), 151.

34. Peter Meinhold, *Modern Europe*, (Philadelphia: Westminster, 1963), 170.

35. F. C. Mather, *The British Laymen in Modern Times* (Philadelphia: Westminster, 1963), 216.

36. Howard Grimes, T*he United States,* (Philadelphia: Westminster, 1963), 245.

37. Ibid.

Empowerment and Entitlement

38. Edward H. Hamnet, *The Gathered and Scattered Church: Equipping Believers for the 21st Century*, (Macon: Smyth Helwys, 1999), 30.

39. Ibid., pg 63.

40. Ibid., pg. 64.

41. Ibid., pg. 65.

42. Sherman L. Young Sr., *Calling The House To Order,* (Chicago, Illinois, Conyers, Ga, Harvest International Publishers), 49.

43. Bishop Larry Trotter, *Dangers of Titles,* (audiocassette) Sweet Holly Spirit Full Gospel Church.

44. George O. McCalep, Jr., *Sin in the House* (Lithonia: Orman Press, 1999), 48.

45. Randy Frazee, "Leading Volunteers," *Christianity Today Magazine*, Spring 1999, 109.

46. John Ortberg, "The Disciple's Dilemma," *Christianity Today*, Spring 2000, 28.

47. Ibid.

48. Sherman Young, *Calling the House to Order,* (Conyers: Harvest Testament Publishers, 2001), 57.

The Polishing of a Pearl

49. Wallace Charles Smith, *The Church in the Life of the Black Family*, (Valley Forge: Judson Press, 1985) pg. 22.

50. Ibid., 4.

51. Ibid.

52. Ibid., 5.

53. Ibid.

54. Dewitt T. Smith, *Putting Laypeople to Work*, 21.

55. John H. Walker, *A Fresh Look at the New Testament Deacon*, (Lithonia: Orman Press, 2000), 27.

The Laity in the New Millennium

56. Hans Ruedi Weber, *The Rediscovery of the Laity in the Economical Movement,* (Philadelphia: Westminster Press, 1963), 388.

57. Ibid., 389.

58. Don Fortune and Katie Fortune, *Discover Your God-Given Gifts,* (Grand Rapids: Chosen Books, 1987), 62.

59. Leighton Ford, *Transforming Leadership* (Downers Grove: Intervarsity, 1993), 20–23.

60. C. Gene Wilkes, *Jesus on Leadership,* (Nashville: LifeWay Press, 1997), 9–25.

61. Robert Greenleaf, *Servant Leadership*, (New York: Paulist Press, 1977), 7.

62. Ibid.

63. James Nouzes and Barry Posner, *Credibility: How Leaders Gain and Lose It*, (San Francisco: Josey-Bass, 1993), 31.

64. Shelia Murray Bethel, *Making a Difference: 12 Qualities That Make You a Leader,* (New York: Berkley Publishing Group, 1990), 16–19.

65. Ibid.

66. J. Robert Clinton, *The Making of a Leader,* (Colorado Springs: NAV Press, 1988), 182–201.

67. John C. Maxwell, *Developing the Leader Within You*, (Nashville: Thomas Nelson Publishing, 1973), 139, 197.

68. John C. Maxwell, *Developing the Leaders Around You,* (Nashville: Thomas Nelson Publishing, 1995), 83–89.

69. Calvin Miller, *The Empowered Leader,* (Nashville, Tennessee: Broadman and Hollman, 1995), 31.

70. Phillip V. Lewis, *Transformational Leadership,* (Nashville: Broadman & Holman Publishers, 1996), 107–109.

71. J. Allen Blair, "How Do You Rate?" *Glad Tiding Newsletter* (September 1998), 1–3.

72. Ibid.

Bibliography

Bethel, Shelia Murray. *Making a Difference: 12 Qualities That Make You a Leader.* New York: Berkley Publishing Group, 1990.

Blair, J. Allen. How Do You Rate? *Glad Tiding Newsletter,* September 1998.

Brook, Christopher N. L. *The Church of the Middle-Ages.* Philadelphia: Westminister Press, 1963.

Cheney, C. R. *From Becket to Langton,* Manchester: 1956.

Clinton, Robert J. *The Making of a Leader.* Colorado Springs: NAV Press, 1988.

Ford, Leighton. *Transforming Leadership.* Downers Grove: Intervarsity, 1963.

Fortune, Don, and Katie Fortune, *Discover Your God-Given Gifts.* Grand Rapids: Chosen Books, 1987.

Frazee, Randy. Leading Volunteers. *Christianity Today Magazine,* Spring 1999.

Frend, William H. C. *The Church of the Roman Empire.* Philadelphia: Westminister Press, 1963.

Greenleaf, Robert. *Servant Leadership.* New York: Paulist Press, 1977.

Grimes, Howard. *The United States*. Philadelphia: Westiminister Press, 1963.

Guns, Geoffrey. *Spiritual Leadership*. Lithonia: Orman Press, 2000.

Hammett, Edward H. *Gathered and Scattered Church: Equipping Believers for 21st Century*. Macon: Smyth Helwys, 1999.

Habecker, Eugene B. *Leading with a Follower's Heart*. Wheaton: Scripture Press, 1990.

Lewis, Phillip V. *Transformational Leadership: A New Model for Total Church Involvement*. Nashville: Broadman & Holman Publishers, 1996.

Massey Jr., Floyd, and Samuel Berry Mckinney. *Church Administration in the Black Perspective*. Valley Forge: Judson Press, 1976.

Mather, F. C. *The British Laymen in Modern Times*. Philadelphia: Westminister Press, 1963.

Maxwell, John C. *Developing the Leader Within You*. Nashville: Thomas Nelson Publishers, 1973.

———*Developing the Leaders Around You*. Nashville: Thomas Nelson Publishing, 1995.

McCalep Jr., George O. *Sin in the House*, Lithonia: Orman Press, 1999.

Meinhold, Peter. *Modern Europe*. Philadelphia: Westminister Press, 1963.

Miller, Calvin. *The Empowered Leader*. Nashville: Broadman & Holman Publisher, 1995.

Nouzes, James, and Barry Posner. *Credibility: How Leaders Gain and Lose It, Why People Demand It*. San Francisco: Josey-Bass, 1993.

Ortberg, John. The Disciple's Dilemma. *Christianity Today Magazine,* Spring 2000.

Perry, Lloyd. *Getting the Church on Target*. Chicago: Moody Press, 1977.

Rupp, Gorden E. *The Age of Reformation,* Philadelphia: Westminister Press, 1963.

Sanders, Oswald J. *Spiritual Leadership*. Chicago: Moody Press, 1967.

Schmidt, Martin. *The Continent of Europe*. Philadelphia: Westminister Press, 1963.

Smith, Dewitt T. *Putting Laypeople to Work*. Atlanta: Hope Publishing House, 1989.

Smith, Wallace Charles. *The Church in the Life of the Black Family*. Valley Forge: Judson Press, 1985.

Thomas, E. L. *Guide to Successful Leadership*. Milwaukee: Calvary Witnessing Voice.

Walker, John H. *A Fresh Look at the New Testament Deacon*. Lithonia: Orman Press, 2000.

Weber, Hans Ruedi and Neil Stephen Charles. *The Layman in Christian History*. Philadelphia: Westminister Press, 1963.

Weber, Hans Ruedi. *The Rediscovery of the Laity in the Economical Movement*. Philadelphia: Westminister Press, 1963.

Wilkes, C. Gene. *Jesus on Leadership*. Nashville: Lifeway Press, 1997.

Williams, George Hunston. *The Ancient Church*. Philadelphia: Westminster press, 1963.

Young, Sherman L. Sr., *Calling the House to Order*. Chicago: Harvest International Press, 2001.

About the Author

John H. Walker was born to the late Leforice Walker, Sr. and Inez Walker in Coosa County, Alabama. He is married to the former Rosie Knight. They have two children, Janetta Olivia and John II, and one grandson, Johnathan Lamar.

Dr. Walker accepted Christ as his personal Savior in 1978 while serving in the armed forces. He was called into the ministry in 1981, and licensed to preach by the New Light Baptist Church.

He earned a master of divinity degree from Shaw Divinity School, Raleigh, North Carolina and a bachelor of arts degree from Shaw University, both of which he graduated Magna Cum Laude. He received theological and Bible degrees from Greensboro Bible College where he was class valedictorian. He also holds a doctor of ministry degree in christian leadership from Gordon Conwell Theological Seminary.

Dr. Walker is a certified instructor for the Southern Baptist Seminary Extension Program and National Baptist Congress of Christian Education Convention.

He is an adjunct professor at Shaw University Cape Center in Kannapolis, North Carolina. He serves on the Equity Committee of the Charlotte Mecklenburg Schools and with the Central Carolina Collective Banking Group, a group of banks that partner with churches and communities to create empowerment.

Under the leading of the Holy Spirit, Dr. Walker became pastor of Macedonia Baptist Church in Charlotte, North Carolina in 1992. Under his leadership, Macedonia has grown spiritually, numerically, and financially. Many new ministries have been created to minister to people both inside and outside of the church, and to foster christian leadership.

Dr. Walker is a visionary leader who has been commissioned to make a difference in this millennium. His burden for the absence of black men in the church and society resulted in the Holy Spirit leading him to research, document and expound on the issue in his book, *The Role of the Church in the Reclaiming of the Black Male*. His book, *A Fresh Look at the New Testament Deacon,* is used in many churches throughout the country as a tool for training deacons and building deacon ministries. Dr. Walker is called upon frequently to develop seminars, instruct convention courses, and lecture.

www.ingramcontent.com/pod-product-compliance
Lightning Source LLC
LaVergne TN
LVHW041110090826
845145LV00003BA/895

* 9 7 8 1 8 9 1 7 7 3 6 2 4 *